Escape from the Edge

THE AZRIELI SERIES OF HOLOCAUST SURVIVOR MEMOIRS: PUBLISHED TITLES

ENGLISH TITLES

William Tannenzapf, *Memories from the Abyss/* Renate Krakauer, *But I Had a Happy Childhood*

Elsa Thon, *If Only It Were Fiction*

Agnes Tomasov, *From Generation to Generation*

Joseph Tomasov, *From Loss to Liberation*

Sam Weisberg, *Carry the Torch/* Johnny Jablon, *A Lasting Legacy*

Leslie Vertes, *Alone in the Storm*

Anka Voticky, *Knocking on Every Door*

Escape from the Edge

Morris Schnitzer

THE AZRIELI FOUNDATION · www.azrielifoundation.org

A version of Morris Schnitzer's memoir was previously published as *My Three Selves*. We thank Morris Schnitzer and Lugus Publications for permitting us to publish this revised edition of his story.

Cover and book design by Mark Goldstein; Maps on pages xxx–xxxi by Deborah Crowle; Endpaper maps by Martin Gilbert; Photos on page 164 courtesy The Ghetto Fighters' House Museum, Israel/ The Photo Archive; Photo of the prison in Arbois, France, on page 165 courtesy of Roger Gibey; Translation of Swiss archival documents by Jean-Philippe Bouriette.

LIBRARY AND ARCHIVES CANADA CATALOGUING IN PUBLICATION

Escape from the Edge/ Morris Schnitzer.
    Schnitzer, Morris, 1922–2020, author. Azrieli Foundation, publisher.
Azrieli series of Holocaust survivor memoirs; XII
Previously published in 2002 under the title: My three selves: a memoir.
Canadiana (print) 20210101598 · Canadiana (ebook) 20210101601
ISBN 9781989719114 (softcover) · ISBN 9781989719183 (HTML)
LCSH: Schnitzer, Morris, 1922– LCSH: Jewish children in the Holocaust — Germany — Biography. LCSH: Jews, German — Netherlands — Biography. LCSH: Holocaust, Jewish (1939–1945) — Personal narratives. LCGFT: Autobiographies.

LCC D804.196 .S35 2021   DDC 940.53/18092 — dc23

PRINTED IN CANADA

The Azrieli Foundation's Holocaust Survivor Memoirs Program

Naomi Azrieli, Publisher

Jody Spiegel, Program Director
Arielle Berger, Managing Editor
Catherine Person, Manager and Editor of French Translations
Catherine Aubé, Editor of French Translations
Matt Carrington, Editor
Devora Levin, Editor and Special Projects Coordinator
Stephanie Corazza, Historian and Manager of Academic Initiatives
Marc-Olivier Cloutier, Manager of Education Initiatives
Elin Beaumont, Community and Education Initiatives
Elizabeth Banks, Digital Asset Curator and Archivist

Mark Goldstein, Art Director
Bruno Paradis, Layout, French-Language Editions

Contents

Series Preface: In their own words. . .

In telling these stories, the writers have liberated themselves. For so many years we did not speak about it, even when we became free people living in a free society. Now, when at last we are writing about what happened to us in this dark period of history, knowing that our stories will be read and live on, it is possible for us to feel truly free. These unique historical documents put a face on what was lost, and allow readers to grasp the enormity of what happened to six million Jews — one story at a time.

David J. Azrieli, C.M., C.Q., M.Arch
Holocaust survivor and founder, The Azrieli Foundation

Since the end of World War II, approximately 40,000 Jewish Holocaust survivors have immigrated to Canada. Who they are, where they came from, what they experienced and how they built new lives for themselves and their families are important parts of our Canadian heritage. The Azrieli Foundation's Holocaust Survivor Memoirs Program was established in 2005 to preserve and share the memoirs written by those who survived the twentieth-century Nazi genocide of the Jews of Europe and later made their way to Canada. The memoirs encourage readers to engage thoughtfully and critically with the complexities of the Holocaust and to create meaningful connections with the lives of survivors.

Millions of individual stories are lost to us forever. By preserving the stories written by survivors and making them widely available to a broad audience, the Azrieli Foundation's Holocaust Survivor Memoirs Program seeks to sustain the memory of all those who perished at the hands of hatred, abetted by indifference and apathy. The personal accounts of those who survived against all odds are as different as the people who wrote them, but all demonstrate the courage, strength, wit and luck that it took to prevail and survive in such terrible adversity. The memoirs are also moving tributes to people — strangers and friends — who risked their lives to help others, and who, through acts of kindness and decency in the darkest of moments, frequently helped the persecuted maintain faith in humanity and courage to endure. These accounts offer inspiration to all, as does the survivors' desire to share their experiences so that new generations can learn from them.

The Holocaust Survivor Memoirs Program collects, archives and publishes select survivor memoirs and makes the print editions available free of charge to educational institutions and Holocaust-education programs across Canada. They are also available for sale online to the general public. All revenues to the Azrieli Foundation from the sales of the Azrieli Series of Holocaust Survivor Memoirs go toward the publishing and educational work of the memoirs program.

～

The Azrieli Foundation would like to express appreciation to the following people for their invaluable efforts in producing this book: Jean-Philippe Bouriette, Judith Clark, Adam Dodek, Mark Duffus (Maracle Inc.), Roger Gibey, Tilman Lewis, Jean Neyroud, Susan Roitman, and Margie Wolfe & Emma Rodgers of Second Story Press.

Editorial Note

The following memoir contains terms, concepts and historical references that may be unfamiliar to the reader. English translations of foreign-language words and terms have been added to the text, and parentheses have been used to include the names and locations of present-day towns and cities when place names have changed. The editors of this memoir have worked to maintain the author's voice and stay true to the original narrative while maintaining historical accuracy. Explanatory footnotes have been added for clarification or to provide key information for understanding the text. General information on major organizations, significant historical events and people, geographical locations, religious and cultural terms, and foreign-language words and expressions that will help give context to the events described in the text can be found in the glossary beginning on page 145.

Introduction

This is a remarkable story of survival against the odds — of Morris Schnitzer's odyssey in occupied Western Europe during the Nazi occupation. What makes his narrative compelling is that he manages to negotiate the myriad hazards of life on the run with very little outside help — relying on his instincts to make the right decisions and learning from his mistakes.

Morris's father, Hermann, had been part of the mass migration of Jews from Tsarist Russia and the Austro-Hungarian Empire in the decades before World War I. The majority left Europe for North America, but a significant number settled in Western European states and formed the basis for the Eastern European Orthodox Jewish communities in major cities there. Emigrating from the Galician town of Rożniatów in 1908 when he was only fourteen years old, Hermann travelled to Germany and began earning a living, like many of his contemporaries, by peddling goods door to door. Unlike his contemporaries, and his father before him, he rapidly moved on from this rather marginal existence to establishing himself as a wholesaler and was soon earning enough to bring his brothers and sisters to join him in Germany.

Hermann's loyalty to his adopted country was completed when he enlisted in the German armed forces during World War I, seeing action on the Eastern Front and spending some time in Russian captivity as a prisoner of war. Returning to an economically shattered Germany at the end of the war, he nevertheless established a successful retail business, choosing to settle not in one of the major urban Jewish centres but in the coal-mining town of Wattenscheid in the Ruhr Valley. Here his family was part of a very small and disparate Jewish community, but ostensibly well-integrated into the locality. He contracted a marriage with Rosa Heller on a visit to Rożniatów (now part of Poland) in 1921 and brought his wife and mother-in-law back to Germany. His three sons, Morris (1922), Edmund (1923) and Benno (1925), were born in quick succession and brought up largely by their devout grandmother — ensuring they were all given a thorough grounding in Orthodox Judaism.

Despite the political and economic turmoil of the times, Hermann's business enterprise thrived, and he was active in both German Social-Democratic Party and Zionist politics. The latter affiliation was more common among the 20 per cent of Eastern European Jews in the country than among their assimilated German Jewish counterparts. Morris recalls that his father not only supported Zionism but was keen to emigrate to Palestine himself and was only dissuaded by his wife's attachment to Germany. The narrative of the early Nazi years after 1933 reflects some of the wider history, with an uncle in Bochum being severely beaten by Nazi thugs, but there is no mention of the April 1, 1933, boycott that affected so many Jewish retail businesses. In apparent contradiction of Nazi aims, Jewish businesses continued to operate and also profited from the general economic recovery after 1933 if they avoided the attention of Nazi zealots and antisemitic local government officials.[1] While living in a town with only a few Jewish families, and thus easily identifiable by local Nazis, the Schnitzers do

---

1   For a detailed discussion, see Avraham Barkai, *From Boycott to Annihilation: The Economic Struggle of German Jews, 1933–1943* (Hanover NH and London: University Press of New England, 1989), 13–109.

not seem to have fallen victim to the low-level discrimination and persecution suffered by so many of their co-religionists in 1933 and 1934.

Over time, however, the discrimination did increase. Morris remained at the *Gymnasium* (high school) in Gelsenkirchen until 1937 when antisemitic pressures forced him out and he joined his younger brother at a Jewish *Gymnasium* in Berlin. This movement from towns and villages to the anonymity of a big city was a common response from many Jews after the increased street violence across the country carried out by the SA in the early spring and summer of 1935, the imposition of the Nuremberg Laws after September 1935 and the increasing pressure for the "Aryanization" of Jewish businesses thereafter.[2] In Berlin, Morris felt safer and reacquainted himself with Zionism. By this stage, it was becoming clear that conditions for Jews in Germany were only likely to worsen. Like many of his co-religionists, Hermann was torn between his loyalty to the country, holding onto his material possessions and refusing to be intimidated on the one hand, and the realization that exile might be the only long-term option on the other. These were common enough emotions among the many Jews who thought of themselves primarily as Germans and who could not understand the regime's sustained program of discrimination and the unpunished violence of its supporters.[3]

Hermann rejected an offer of help to resettle in Australia in 1935, but there were plans to expedite the emigration of their children as soon as possible. In the meantime, one uncle had already left for Palestine and another was deported back to Poland with his wife and youngest son, presumably in the *Aktion* that took place in October 1938. This was a major watershed for many of the country's Polish

2 Peter Longerich, *Holocaust: The Nazi Persecution and Murder of the Jews* (Oxford: Oxford University Press, 2010), 54–56.

3 Jürgen Matthäus and Mark Roseman, *Jewish Responses to Persecution, Volume 1, 1933–1938* (Lanham MD: AltaMira Press/USHMM, 2010), 87–88.

Jews and was prompted by the Warsaw government attempting to strip them of their nationality, which led the Gestapo to round up and expel some 18,000 people to the Polish frontier on the night of October 28 and into the morning of October 29, where around 8,000 were denied entry and left in no man's land near Zbąszyń, with neither Germany nor Poland willing to accept responsibility for them.[4]

For Hermann Schnitzer's immediate family, the so-called Kristallnacht (Night of Broken Glass) pogrom on November 9 to 10, 1938, was the watershed, as it was for so many Jews in Germany. Although Morris and his younger brother saw little of the immediate destruction in their part of Berlin, a frantic phone call from their mother brought them home to the charred ruins of the family business and their immediate arrest — a fate that had already befallen their father. Across the country, at least 30,000 male Jews were arrested in the hours and days after the pogrom and taken to concentration camps, primarily Dachau, Buchenwald and Sachsenhausen.[5]

In the days and weeks that followed, Rosa Schnitzer worked tirelessly to obtain her husband's and sons' release — a feature of this period where the male heads of households had been arrested en masse and the role of decision-maker passed to women whose traditional role was in the private sphere. With her active involvement in the family business, Rosa was perhaps more prepared than most of her contemporaries for this new and unaccustomed role. Her sons had not been sent to Sachsenhausen because it was already overcrowded, and the younger Edmund was released after two weeks (possibly on account of his age); Morris followed two weeks later, but only after his mother had arranged a place for him on the so-called Kindertransport. After the British government had agreed to

---

4   Barkai, *From Boycott to Annihilation*, 133.
5   Walter Pehle, *November 1938: From "Kristallnacht" to Genocide* (London: Bloomsbury, 1990); Rita Thalmann and Emmanuel Feinermann, *Crystal Night 9–10 November 1938* (London: Thames and Hudson, 1974), 117; Longerich, *Holocaust*, 112.

waive certain entry requirements for unaccompanied Jewish children in the aftermath of Kristallnacht, Geertruida (Truus) Wijsmuller-Meijer, a Dutch social activist who had already been involved in getting children out of Germany, was recruited by the newly formed British Refugee Children's Movement to negotiate the first mass transport with Adolf Eichmann in Vienna. Ultimately, the organization managed to evacuate more than 10,000 children from Germany and Austria — with most of them going to the United Kingdom. Smaller numbers were taken in by France and Belgium, while Morris Schnitzer was one of around 1,500 children who were selected to go to the Netherlands.[6]

In the Netherlands, the children were supported by the Dutch Jewish refugee organizations but under the overall control of the Dutch authorities, whose attitude toward them was little better than sufferance. Morris and some of his contemporaries were something of an anomaly as the Dutch had been expecting small children rather than adolescents. As a result, they were moved on many occasions and closely monitored. Internment camps, quarantine camps, disused orphanages and out-of-season youth hostels were all used as accommodations. Here he stayed until war broke out in September 1939 — still able to write and even telephone his parents and occasionally visiting an aunt in Maastricht, but otherwise kept in complete idleness. It was this aunt who attempted to get the rest of the family out of Germany by sending a car to collect them, but Hermann — now released but ill and weakened from the treatment meted out by the SS concentration camp guards — stubbornly refused to leave without proper authorization, and the scheme collapsed. Like many of his coreligionists, he saw his patriotism and military service as touchstones

---

6 See Truus Wijsmuller-Meijer, *Truus Wijsmuller-Meijer: Herinneringen van een verzetsvrouw, 1938–1945* (Amsterdam: Lida Boukris-Jong, 2017); Truus Wijsmuller-Meijer, *Geen tijd voor tranen* (Amsterdam: van Kampen, 1961).

that would somehow protect him — despite what he had seen and experienced in Sachsenhausen.

It was more than a year after his arrival, and after war had broken out in Europe, that Morris received residential status in the Netherlands and was freed from the internment system — but only on condition that he enrol at the Mizrachi Zionist training institute (*hachshara*) based in the Friesian town of Franeker.[7] As had been the case throughout the 1930s, the Dutch authorities were keen to expedite the re-emigration of as many refugee Jews from Germany as possible. From there, Morris was sent out to farms to learn the agricultural skills that would qualify him for entry to Palestine as a settler but, like many of his contemporaries, his urban upbringing left him ill-prepared for agricultural life. Nevertheless, he stuck it out, even after the German occupation of the country.

On hearing about the invasion on May 10, 1940, and fearing like so many other Jews what German rule would entail for them, Morris and a fellow trainee fled Franeker with the intention of reaching the North Sea ports.[8] However, they never managed to join the throng of people jamming the roads and besieging the ports of IJmuiden and Rotterdam in the chaotic days that followed. Cycling westwards but without their identity papers, they were soon apprehended by Dutch soldiers who assumed they were German fifth-columnists.[9] Imprisoned with known Dutch and German Nazis, the two were then "liberated" by the advancing Wehrmacht, congratulated on their survival and given a free ride back to Amsterdam.

---

7   See Dan Michman, "Zionist Youth Movements in Holland and Belgium and Their Activities during the Shoah" in *Zionist Youth Movements during the Shoah*, eds. Asher Cohen and Yehoyakim Cochavi (New York: Peter Lang, 1995), 145–171.

8   Peter Romijn, "De Oorlog (1940-1945)" in *Geschiedenis van de Joden in Nederland*, eds. J.C.H. Blom et al. (Amsterdam: Balans, 1995), 315–316.

9   Lou de Jong, *The German Fifth Column in the Second World War* (London: Routledge and Kegan Paul, 1956), 182–196.

Arriving in an almost deserted city, they behaved in much the same way as the rest of the Dutch population. After the initial shock of invasion, there was a rapid resumption of everyday life as people returned home and resumed their jobs. Morris and his friend returned unmolested to Franeker, where their agricultural and religious training continued. In the first months there were few antisemitic measures enacted by the incoming Germans, but Jews were forced to register and were expelled from government and civil service positions. In February 1941, disturbances in Jewish quarters of Amsterdam instigated by Dutch National Socialists were met with local retaliation and a further German crackdown, which in turn prompted a nationwide general strike involving more than 300,000 people that lasted for two days before being suppressed. These events led directly to the creation of the Jewish Council in Amsterdam, but little of this had much impact on life in the training camp in rural Friesland.

Perhaps surprisingly, links to the outside world remained intact, with Morris receiving a Red Cross card from his brother, who had reached England but was subsequently arrested as an enemy alien after May 1940 and shipped to Canada, where he was interned at the Fredericton internment camp. Morris took comfort from the fact that his brother, although interned, was well away from Europe, and had, unbeknownst to him, also avoided the fate of similar internees on board the SS *Arandora Star*, which had been torpedoed and sunk by a German submarine on July 2, 1940.[10] Less reassuring were the letters from his parents, now effectively isolated and ghettoized in Dortmund, Germany. Phone calls were no longer possible, but a censored mail system still functioned, and Morris could read between the lines that his parents and youngest brother were barely existing with no means of improving their situation.

---

10 For detail on British policy toward its internees, see Peter and Leni Gilman, *Collar the Lot! How Britain Interned and Expelled Its Wartime Refugees* (London: Quartet, 1980).

His peaceful existence at Franeker came to an end in October 1941 when the Germans aided by Dutch police mounted a raid and arrested all the trainees — using the excuse that they had been hoarding food.[11] This was part of an action directed against German Jews who were required to register for "voluntary" emigration — as was evident when the Dutch Jews among them were subsequently released.[12]

Morris managed to escape with one of his comrades, and the two of them made their way to the Mizrachi headquarters in Amsterdam. Directed to the offices of the Jewish Council, they were told to give themselves up as the Gestapo had threatened to send all the trainees to Westerbork.[13] This behaviour by the Jewish Council officials was typical of their responses to German demands — namely to accede "lest something worse befall" (*om erger te voorkomen*) — a phrase that would become infamous once the widespread arrests and deportations of Jews began in the summer of 1942. Appalled by their acquiescence, Morris received help from the Mizrachi movement to go underground — what the Dutch called *onderduiken* — and was initially hidden in the homes of wealthy Jewish families who probably thought they had less to fear or thought they could buy their way out of trouble. Without viable papers and on the run from the authorities, Morris can be counted among the first cohort of Jews in the Netherlands to choose illegality as a survival strategy. At this stage,

---

11 Jacques Presser, *Ondergang: De vervolging en verdelging van het Nederlandse Jodendom, 1940–1945*, Vol. I, (s'Gravenhage: Staatsuitgeverij, 1977), 449; Hans Schippers, *Westerweel Group: Non-conformist Resistance Against Nazi Germany: A Joint Rescue Effort of Dutch Idealists and Dutch-German Zionists* (Boston/Berlin: De Gruyter, 2019), 91.

12 Bob Moore, *Victims and Survivors: The Nazi Persecution of the Jews in the Netherlands, 1940–1945* (London: Arnold, 1996), 84–85.

13 Westerbork had been established as a refugee camp in 1939 and even in 1941 was still controlled by the Dutch authorities. Only in July 1942 was it formally taken over by the SS as a *Durchgangslager* (transit camp) and became the primary point of departure for the trains to Auschwitz and Sobibor.

the processes of exclusion and pauperization of the Jews was already well underway, with a raft of legislation restricting their ability to earn a living. At the same time, there was increasing pressure on the Dutch unemployed to work in Germany, on pain of losing any state support for their families. The growing number of Jews deprived of their livelihoods could not be sent to Germany, but to make sure they did not get preferential treatment they were confined to labour camps inside the Netherlands.[14] Those incarcerated in this way became some of the earliest victims of the deportations that began in July 1942.

The first call-ups sent to Jews in Amsterdam and elsewhere for "labour service in the East" were very soon replaced by nighttime German and Dutch police raids on Jewish neighbourhoods. Morris's experience of these raids together with the shortages of food and increasing insecurity in the city led him to find another escapee from Franeker who had an uncle living in Brussels, and together they managed to cross the Belgian border. Travelling without valid papers, they seem to have been extremely lucky in avoiding identity checks on the railways but knew enough to cross the border on foot via the so-called green frontier to avoid controls there. Once in Brussels, he and his colleague found refuge with the uncle and were able to obtain Belgian identity documents without much difficulty. Registration and control of the Jewish population in Belgium had been much less rigorous than in the Netherlands, a function of limited SS presence there and little overt cooperation from the Belgian authorities in matters pertaining to the Jewish question. The Jews also benefited from a nascent self-help organization, the Comité de Défense des Juifs (CDJ), which was linked to a wider non-Jewish resistance movement, the Front de l'Indépendence/Onafhankelijkheidsfront, with the former acting as an effective counterweight to the German-sponsored representative organization, the Association des Juifs de Belgique.[15] The story also

---

14 Moore, *Victims and Survivors*, 85–86.

15 The CDJ had arisen from welfare organizations set up in the inter-war period to

indicates how resistance links to cooperative local government officials allowed fugitives like Morris and his friend to obtain ostensibly real documents that masked their Jewish identities.[16]

Continuing their journey toward Switzerland through France, the pair made mistakes that might under other circumstances have been fatal — for example, carrying phylacteries and attending a synagogue service in Nancy where they stood out from the local congregation. However, they also developed a technique for minimizing the danger in asking for help, by going into church confession booths. By their own admission, this always brought at least a meal and sometimes advice on where to go next. This strategy served them well, and they were able to cross unaided into Swiss territory, but here their luck ran out. Swiss policy toward (Jewish) refugees had always been highly restrictive but became positively draconian after the summer of 1942, although ultimately around 15,000 were admitted and interned.[17] Schnitzer and his companion were unlucky and instead of being interned, the two were conducted back to the French frontier under threat that if they were ever found on Swiss soil again, they would be handed over directly to the Gestapo.

Back in France, Morris then tried to traverse the demarcation line into the unoccupied zone of France, where he thought conditions for Jews were better, but was arrested by a German patrol. Here again, he may have been unlucky in his choice of crossing point, as other

---

help Jewish immigrants from Eastern Europe, who made up 95 per cent of the entire Jewish population of the country by 1940. See José Gotovitch, "Resistance Movements and the 'Jewish Question,'" in *Belgium and the Holocaust: Jews, Belgians, Germans*, ed. Dan Michman (Jerusalem: Yad Vashem, 1998), 280–285.

16 Ahlrich Meyer and Insa Meinen, "La Belgique, pays de transit: Juifs fugitifs en Europe occidentale au temps des déportations de 1942," *Bijdragen tot de eigentijdse geschiedenis (1930/1960)* 20 (2008): 145–194.

17 Ruth Fivaz-Silbermann, "The Swiss Reaction to the Nazi Genocide: Active Refusal, Passive Help" in *Resisting Genocide: The Multiple Forms of Rescue*, eds. Jacques Semelin et al. (Oxford: Oxford University Press, 2014).

locations were easier to negotiate, sometimes with the help of local government officials.[18] Sentenced to three months in jail for trying to cross the border illegally, he was moved several times and survived beatings, starvation and deportation back to Belgium without his true identity being revealed. Freed from the notorious Saint-Gilles prison in Brussels but with no contacts or knowledge of the city, he had enough sense to avoid the obvious trap of having any dealings with the Association des Juifs de Belgique. Morris found his way to a non-Jewish Austrian couple he had met on his first visit to the city. In the interim, the husband had been arrested and the wife had become heavily involved in resistance activities and introduced him to the Witte Brigade (White Brigade). This group had been founded as the Geuzengroep in Antwerp in late 1940 by teacher Marcel Louette and had spread to other towns and cities, primarily in Flanders, organizing demonstrations, publishing underground newspapers and sheltering Jews and other fugitives before becoming involved in direct actions against the German occupation. The group developed into a fully fledged active resistance organization with branches in various towns and cities. Morris joined the group in Brussels as an act of survival and to take the fight to the Germans. With little to lose, he became involved in all manner of armed resistance actions.

Such activities engendered severe German reprisals, including the shooting of civilian hostages — something that made the armed resistance unpopular with the local population and made his group a prime target for the Gestapo. The group's plans to evacuate to England in February 1943 were foiled when their hideout was raided, although the idea that a group of fifteen resistance fighters could actually be flown to England in early 1943 seems somewhat fanciful. The fact that he escaped and avoided injury is little short of miraculous, but his narrow escape precluded any further active involvement

18 Michael R. Marrus and Robert O. Paxton, *Vichy France and the Jews* (Stanford CA: Stanford University Press, 1995), 148–149.

in the resistance, and he was forced to go further underground. Here again, his Austrian resistance worker came to his rescue by providing a further contact that allowed Morris to escape into the countryside. Although the CDJ helped support some 12,000 adult Jews in hiding during the occupation, it does not appear that Morris benefited from this form of help, save perhaps for the provision of an initial placement.

At a time when labour was in extremely short supply, farmers were always on the lookout for additional hands without asking too many questions, and so working for them became a common refuge for young Jewish men and women on the run who had no viable papers but who did not look "too Jewish," not only in Belgium but also in other parts of occupied Western Europe. In exchange for work, the job often provided food and lodging, something of great value for those without access to ration stamps. For the next eighteen months, Morris worked on at least three farms, but conditions were poor, and employers were keen to extract the maximum amount of value from their employees for the minimum outlay. Labourers "living in" were often accommodated in barns and outhouses and were seldom, if ever, invited into the farmhouses. Discontent could lead to fugitives leaving the relative safety of the farm and taking enormous risks in travelling and looking for work, and many were captured on the road during the later stages of the war.

Morris's last farm job highlights some of the contradictions of life on the run. The farmer treated him reasonably well and only asked him a couple of times for his papers — ostensibly only so that he could be legitimately registered as "essential" and thus not liable for forced labour in Germany. His employer was obviously well thought of in the locality but also had connections with the Germans, and there were regular visits from the military commander in Liège. This, of itself, might have been enough to condemn the farmer when the Germans were driven out and the local resistance began meting out summary justice, but he was saved by Morris's testimony — that despite his links to the Germans, he had also been a rescuer. As in so many other instances, the distinctions between collaboration and resistance were seldom clear-cut.

If anything, Morris's postwar history was just as remarkable. Travelling back to Brussels, he soon found work with the Allied occupation forces as a labourer and then undertook tests to become an interpreter. With fluency in German, French and Dutch as well as good English, he was adopted by the Americans — testimony to the shortages of skilled communications personnel within the 21st Army Group as the front moved into Germany. By his own admission he was keen to take the fight to the Germans in revenge for the fate of his family but was usually kept away from the fighting. His role as an interpreter meant he was involved in the interrogation of captured German service personnel — both Wehrmacht and SS. As he makes clear, this was done primarily to extract military intelligence rather than to investigate war crimes. Allied policy made distinctions between the German army and the SS, where the former was considered to have fought within the rules of war and the latter was seen as a criminal organization and responsible with the Nazi Party for the atrocities committed by the regime. While this provided a convenient and perhaps necessary distinction for the Allies at the time, it meant that many soldiers were never investigated. This gave rise to the myth of the "clean" Wehrmacht in the West, which was only challenged several decades later.

After the war ended, Morris became increasingly disenchanted with his role as a peacetime interpreter and had no desire to stay in Germany. Having been legally admitted to the Netherlands, going back there represented his best chance of re-establishing himself and fulfilling his ambition of going to Palestine. Returning to Franeker, he was able to obtain identity papers even though he had been listed as dead by the local authorities in 1942. He was likewise able to obtain a new visa and access to ration cards from officials in Amsterdam. Ostensibly, this was a largely seamless and unremarkable process but Morris's experience contrasts with the treatment meted out by the Dutch authorities to returning German refugee Jews in 1945, when many of them were arrested when they crossed the border and interned with Nazis and collaborators. Nevertheless, Morris did encounter bureaucratic intransigence when he failed to get permission from the Ministry of Social Affairs to marry a Jewish girl who was still a ward of the court — on the grounds that he did not have stable employment (he had rejoined the Mizrachi movement), and later when he tried to obtain identity documents that would allow him to travel — on the grounds that he was not a Dutch national. In the latter case he was able to persuade the police that if they wanted rid of him, the documentation would allow him to leave, whatever the rules were.

Many Dutch Jewish survivors of the Holocaust chose emigration to Palestine after the war — their experiences at the hands of the Germans having been compounded by the uncaring attitude of the postwar Dutch authorities and a resurgence of antisemitic undercurrents in the country.[19] Morris Schnitzer would almost certainly have made the same journey had it not been for the persuasive talents of his brother and his strong desire to enhance and complete his education that brought him to Canada in 1947. His memoir is testimony to the myriad choices that those on the run had to make — often at very short notice. While undoubtedly making some astute decisions, as he himself acknowledges, his survival was also down to large slices of luck and marginally different circumstances or decisions on his part could have had fatal consequences.

Bob Moore
Emeritus Professor of History, University of Sheffield
2020

---

19 See Dienke Hondius, *Return: Holocaust Survivors and Dutch Anti-Semitism* (Westport, CT: Praeger, 2003).

Maps

North Sea

UNITED KINGDOM

English Channel

NETHERLANDS

Franeker
Harlingen
Sneek
Westerbork
AMSTERDAM
Gouda
Rotterdam
Deventer
Dieren
De Steeg
GERMANY
Winterswijk
Gelsenkirchen
Wattenscheid
Rhine
Hoorn
Krefeld
Strombeek-Bever
Hasselt
Beek
BRUSSELS
Maastricht
Lille
Tournai
Waterloo
Fexhe-le-Haut-Clocher
Denain
BELGIUM
Koblenz
Mainz
LUXEMBOURG
To Würzburg
PARIS
LUXEMBOURG CITY

Occupied Zone

Nancy
Zone Annexed by Germany
Rhine

Fournet-Blancheroche
Besançon
Belfort
Dijon
Doubs
Maîche
Morteau
BERN
La Chaux-de-Fonds
FRANCE
Arbois
Jura Mountains
SWITZERLAND

Free Zone
Demarcation Line

ITALY

0   50   100 km

© 2021 – The Azrieli Foundation

Legend

—— Borders in 1938	Occupied by Germany in 1940	Occupied by Germany in 1942	Occupied by Italy in 1942

Acknowledgements

The author thanks his late wife, Leah, for insisting that he write this memoir and for transcribing the first draft; his daughter, Eve, for organizing the manuscript and for her afterword; and Seymour Mayne, distinguished Canadian poet, and his wife, Sharon Katz, for their long-term encouragement of this book.

Prologue

In 1941, in a city called Franeker in the Netherlands, I lost my true identity when I fled the Gestapo. About five years later, in the same place, I regained it.

It's difficult to explain the effects of living with a false identity. When I changed my name, I knew that I had to conceal many aspects of my personality. In a sense, I had to cease being the type of person I'd been until then. To achieve this, I censored everything I said and did; I controlled myself every minute. I mumbled or I said nothing so as not to reveal too much of who I was. This was very hard sometimes: people tend to equate silence with unfriendliness and resent it.

With my false identities, I no longer felt German. I couldn't disclose that I had any special knowledge of Germany or personal relationship to Germany. I felt like nothing I had ever been. I had to earn my daily bread by the sweat of my brow at the lowest level of society. Like an actor, I had to play a role — mine was to appear to be dull and crude, without education or refinement. Reading or discussions were banned from my life.

The problem with keeping up my false identities was that I was almost always with other people; I worked and even slept beside other people. And I couldn't afford to give myself away by chattering either in my sleep or when awake. I was concerned that when I was sleeping, someone might get information from me that I wouldn't want to divulge. I was always afraid that someone might question me some day or something might happen to unmask me.

I'd had enough of being someone else. I was tired of withholding so much and expecting to be discovered. I wanted my own identity again.

A Jewish Childhood in Germany

I was born into a Jewish family in Germany in 1922. The old city of Bochum, Westphalia, some forty kilometres east of the Rhine River, was (and is) one of the industrial centres of the Ruhr Valley. Then as now, this area along the Ruhr River had the biggest steel mills in Germany. Steelworks ranged along roadsides in Bochum near the coal mines that fed the coke ovens. A mere ten kilometres from us loomed Essen, one of the major industrial cities of Europe, with the enormous iron- and steel-making plants founded by the Krupp family in the early nineteenth century.

My father, Hermann Schnitzer, had immigrated to Germany in 1908 from Galicia in what was to become Poland. At that time, it was part of the Austro-Hungarian Empire. Europe was a very different place then in many ways. My father was only about fourteen years old, just past his bar mitzvah when he left home on his own.

In Germany, he started out buying and selling produce from farms. Like many Jewish migrants in different corners of the world throughout history, he began as a travelling peddler. At the age of sixteen, when he knew the ropes and had the contacts, he decided to become an egg wholesaler. Even back then a licence was required to sell almost anything in Germany. When my father applied to the bureau and was asked his age, he was told he was too young to be granted a licence. But somehow he acquired this and launched a wholesale business. He was successful from the start. He had exceptional business ability.

His father had moved to Germany before him but was never successful there. Maybe he just couldn't adjust to the conditions or to the language as an older man; life was very different in his native Galicia, where he had spoken Yiddish.

My father adapted readily and did well. His two older brothers, Beryl and Josef, followed him to Germany. Then he brought his sisters, Rosa and Augusta (Gusta), there. Finally, in 1922, after I was born, he brought over his younger brother, Mischel. But my father's mother never left Poland.

During World War 1, my father enlisted in the army. Austria and Germany were allies, and as an Austrian citizen, my father served with German troops in the infantry corps. He fought in several battles on the Eastern Front and was decorated with the Iron Cross. He was taken prisoner in Russia and forced to work in the forests — he was soon in charge of a timber yard; even as a prisoner of war, my father used his talent for management.

After the war he settled back in Germany, land of opportunity. Then in 1921 he made a trip to the place of his birth, a Polish town called Rożniatów (now Rozhniativ in Ukraine) in the Carpathian foothills near Stanisławów (now Ivano-Frankivsk), not far from Czernowitz (now Chernivtsi). He married my mother there and whisked her off to Germany, where she too would flourish in a more challenging and rewarding world.

My mother's family name was Heller. "Berta" was what my father called her, although her given name was Rosa and her Hebrew name was Miriam. She was the only child of Shoshi and Moishe Heller. Moishe was a well-to-do man who had died in 1908. He had been supervising the construction of a building when a wall collapsed on him, crushing his kidneys. Although he had gone for treatment to a hospital in Vienna, the leading medical centre of the world at that time, even the most able doctors couldn't save him. He was buried in the Wiener Zentralfriedhof, the Vienna Central Cemetery. In 1932, my mother journeyed to Vienna to oversee the headstone being placed on his gravesite. After his death my grandmother managed their hardware store in Rożniatów. It was the only establishment of its kind in that sprawling countryside and it prospered. When my parents were married, my grandmother went with them to Germany, and the store closed.

In 1922, when I was born, my father owned a chain of retail shops in the Ruhr district. Three of these shops were in Wattenscheid, an industrial town with a population of about sixty thousand and situated about six kilometres from Bochum. My parents moved us there when I was six weeks old.

Our furniture store in Wattenscheid was located on Hochstrasse, the high street in the upper town. Our shoe store and general clothing store, which sold every conceivable type of clothing, were in the main business district downtown, at opposite ends of Oststrasse. We lived in one of the two large apartments over the clothing store. Many of our neighbours also lived above their shops.

Both my parents worked in the clothing store in Wattenscheid. My mother had grown up in a retail business and was an expert salesperson. Often when I was in the store a customer would come in to buy a single item, such as a pair of pants, and she would sell him a three-piece suit, a shirt and tie, and a hat. He would spend more than he had intended but he would leave the store satisfied!

Our family also included my two younger brothers, Edmund (Eddi), born in 1923, and Benno, born in 1925. We were all raised by our maternal grandmother, Baba Shoshi, who took charge of us children and the housekeeping, assisted by a young live-in maid.

Baba Shoshi was descended from a line of rabbinical scholars, and her chief concern was our Jewish education. She was very religious: she prayed many times each day, and I copied her. From the age of three, I could recite or read Hebrew prayers fluently. I became well advanced in reciting the liturgy.

There were only about a hundred Jews, twenty-five to thirty families, living in Wattenscheid. The Wassermanns were our closest Jewish friends. They lived three or four blocks from us. The Spiegels lived a ten-minute walk away. There was no ghetto, and no segregation of Jews.

Our immediate neighbours were all non-Jews. The pharmacy across from our house belonged to the pharmacist Schulte, a wealthy and nationalistic German who lived there with his family. He had several sons, all of whom were older than me. I grew up with them. Their mother was a haughty woman whose family owned much of the land in Wattenscheid.

Coal mining was the main industry of Wattenscheid. Every day I watched miners head to work with lamps on their helmets. From our home, we could see them descend into the pits.

Most of our customers in our clothing store were miners, and so I got to know many of them and learned about the hazards they faced. They put in long hours of dirty, back-breaking work in narrow, damp, dark suffocating passageways. Their lives were always in danger. Some of the region's miners were Polish in origin and had Polish names. Even the immigrants from Poland had been in Germany for some time; few of them spoke Polish.

I went to school with the children of miners, steelworkers, business owners and professionals. This part of Germany was prosperous: it was industrialized, dynamic, and people earned relatively high wages. I am sure that my father had chosen to live there because the area favoured enterprise — and hard work.

～

I did get to see where my parents were from in Poland when I was young. In 1927, the whole family, including Baba Shoshi, travelled first-class by train to Rożniatów and spent two months in Poland. I was five, Eddi was four and Benno was just a two-year-old toddler. Baba Shoshi's house there, which was also my grandparents' old store, was a beautiful stone building several storeys high, with the large hardware store on the ground floor. It was a strange place. Goods were still on the shelves, even though the store had been closed since my parents' wedding.

During our stay, my father rented a horse-drawn carriage and hired a driver. We drove from village to village through the rolling rural landscape, past well-kept farms and forests with lots of creatures in the wild. There were very few bridges, so the horses had to plunge into the shallow water of rivers and streams to cross them. We were thrilled by this each time; we had never experienced anything like it in Germany.

Wherever we went, my father was received like royalty. Maybe the treatment was due to small-town hospitality and the predictable welcome for a prodigal son. But my father also made bountiful donations to every local synagogue and institution — to his credit and his misfortune, he was never one to be tight with money. His ties to the area were strong, since his mother was still living there with his sister Dina, whose husband had decamped to Brazil by himself in 1922. My father was the sole support of his mother for many years, and of Dina and her three children until 1935. Then my aunt Dina and three cousins also immigrated to Brazil. My father's mother was one of his prime concerns, and he sent money to her every month, no matter the circumstances. His brothers and sisters, apparently, never helped to support her. My parents had heated arguments over this.

I suppose my father was an idealist and a dreamer. But his idealism made a deep impression on me, and it stayed alive in me even when it became tempered with the most bitter doses of reality. He was active in the Socialist Party in Germany and had many friends who were involved in politics. He was also a dedicated Zionist. Whenever world Zionist leaders visited our region, my father met them personally and helped organize their rallies. Not only was he generous in contributing time, energy and money toward Eretz Yisrael, the Land of Israel, but he also hoped to settle there. He often spoke of wanting us to grow up as Jews in Eretz Yisrael.

My father was ready to move to what was then Palestine in 1928. My brothers and I were all preschoolers, and my father was thirty-four years old. At that stage in his life, with a firm financial base, he felt able to pull up roots and branch out in new directions, but my mother balked at moving to Palestine. She was very fond of Germany. She enjoyed German cultural life and wanted her children to have the benefits of German culture and education. She refused to uproot herself and us for a barren, underdeveloped place. And so we stayed. The road to hell is paved with good intentions.

I began to attend school in 1928, when I was six years old. I had tried to go to school once before, to the only local preschool, which was run by Catholics. I had had a nice morning there, but when my grandmother picked me up she asked me what I had learned. I told her we had been singing songs about Jesus, and she decided I wouldn't be going back there and continued to teach me herself at home. But now that I was old enough to go to school, there was more choice. Most schools in our region belonged to one of three systems: Catholic, Protestant or "free" schools.

In the Ruhr Valley, Socialists were politically powerful and ran their own schools, free of religious instruction. The *Freie Schule* in Wattenscheid was called the Lessing Schule, in honour of the great and tolerant eighteenth-century German writer Gotthold Ephraim Lessing. I was a pupil at the Lessing Schule and the only Jewish boy in the class.

The school was in the upper town, near the Catholic school. I endured my first ordeals passing by the Catholic school to get to my school and to return home. On my way home from school each and every day, three or four Catholic boys would be waiting for me. They would jeer at me: *Jude Itzig Nase spitzig!* This well-known rhyme among Germans meant "Izzie the pointed-nose Jew." They would also beat me and pelt me with stones. No classmate ever rallied to help me. Grownups would hurry by, seemingly not realizing what was going on.

A number of times I took refuge in our furniture store, where my uncle Mischel was the manager. I would scuttle inside and pour out to him what was happening, and he would then take me home. My father eventually had one of our office staff escort me to and from school every day.

Sometimes my brothers and I were even stoned by other kids on our outings. We learned to stroll in groups. Then, one day, we threw stones back at our attackers, returning their blows and scaring them off. These incidents all occurred in 1928, when I was in Grade 1. They stopped after that, probably because we fought back!

Throughout my early school years, I was aware of social unrest and business setbacks around me. There were business failures accompanied by increasing unemployment in 1928. Because my father was advancing merchandise on credit to scores of Jewish peddlers from Poland, he lost ruinous sums of money.

The peddlers used to throng our stores every morning, replenishing their stock of goods. Then they would fan out to sell in the region. My father expected these men to pay him for the stock they took, but some of them never did. The arguments my parents had about this were formidable. My mother would say my father was gullible and trusted people too much; he would respond that he was right to trust people.

In 1929, circumstances started to really deteriorate. By 1931–32, most of the peddlers were unable to pay anything because their customers were short of cash. It was the depth of the Depression, and my father was teetering on the verge of bankruptcy.

My mother prevailed on him to stay out of the stores and to let her manage them. He withdrew to a mountain resort in the Black Forest while she set to work. She collected some outstanding debts and reduced the army of peddlers, pared unprofitable goods and services and succeeded in saving the business.

My father was an expansive and impressive personality. He conceived vast schemes and dreams. He had fulfilled these ideas in part, but the times were no longer right for dreamers. By contrast, my mother was a pragmatic, down-to-earth person. She never laboured under illusions. She was a doer who set herself limited aims and accomplished them efficiently.

Meanwhile, Baba Shoshi, after years of murmuring that she hated Germany — "Germans are vulgar," she would complain — suddenly announced one day in 1932 that she was going back to Poland. Soon afterward, she kissed us goodbye. Not long after, we learned that she was ill with cancer. She had gone back to Poland to die.

She had spoken of wanting to be buried in Poland. When we heard of her illness, my father went to spend some time with her. A few months later she was dead. I was heartbroken.

But life went on, and even in sad and uncertain times our family managed to take holidays away from sooty Wattenscheid. My parents usually took vacations separately so that one of them could stay behind to run the stores. Their choice of holiday spots differed: my father preferred to slow down and rest in a quiet environment, while my mother loved the whirl of elegant spas.

I often tagged along with my mother to German resorts, such as her favourites, Bad Ems, or Bad Kreuznach, Bad Neuenahr, Bad Soden or Baden-Baden. She tolerated this because I was obedient and well-behaved — the typical, serious, eldest son. Eddi, on the other hand, was inclined to tear around wildly, breaking glasses and creating havoc. And Benno was simply too small to be taken along.

I loved the setting of the spas. The buildings were usually white or pastel-coloured. The parks were green and fresh, with flowered promenades and clear rivers. It was a blissful change from our coal-black region, and I have always remembered these places with fondness.

～

In 1932, I had also completed the four years of German primary school and began *Gymnasium*, which was then the typical secondary school for boys.

The *Gymnasium* building was closer to our home than the *Freie Schule* had been. I was friendly with many of my non-Jewish classmates: we played soccer together and frequently visited each others' homes. Robert Schulte, the pharmacist's son, was a few years older than I was. I saw him at school every day and sometimes we walked there or back together.

Most of my Jewish education was acquired at home from private teachers. As far back as I remember, my brothers and I were taught both Hebrew and Talmud, the oral law and commentaries on the Torah. Teachers were engaged at considerable expense to instruct us for a few hours two afternoons a week. Since our own Jewish community was so small, they had to come to our house from Essen, a train journey that took an hour each way.

My father also decided that year that my brothers and I should learn English, so we started taking regular private lessons. I don't know what possessed him, since it was not a common view then that English would be a major language of the future. Looking back, I suppose he knew his sons would leave Germany one day. English was, after all, not only the language of the United States, where so many emigrants went, but it was also still the language spoken in Palestine under the British mandate. Whatever his reasons were, he did a great service for me and Eddi by forcing us to learn English from a young age. My knowledge of English would serve me well long before I got to Canada.

We were exposed to a barrage of languages, which we didn't appreciate at the time. At home we spoke Yiddish and German. At school, while I was starting English at home, I started learning Latin from the first year of *Gymnasium*. In third year, I also had French, and in fourth year, English. By that time, my English was relatively well advanced, which was lucky for me because the method of teaching was to plunge us into the classics, such as works by Sir Walter Scott, who haunts me to this day, and then use translation and grammatical explanations to get us through a sea of foreign words. I suspect I was one of the few who could follow the lessons! And then, of course, there were those eternal Hebrew and Talmud lessons.

There were other lessons, besides. For a number of years I studied violin; I played well but wasn't keen on practising. Eddi drew very well and took lessons in sketching from an established artist. My father spent a fortune on our education; there was no limit to it. He had infinite respect for learning. And he knew it was something we could carry with us wherever we might go.

Fanning the Embers

The political climate in 1932 was incredibly tense. There were six million unemployed in Germany. Our region was hit very hard. The Communists were strong in our area, and the Socialists also had large segments of the population supporting them. The Nazis were gaining in strength and were even more militant than the Communists — they were fighting in the open, strutting about and beating people in the streets.

We weren't alarmed by the Nazis, because they weren't in power. They seemed to us more like rowdies and ruffians than a menace to the state. At least this was the picture I got from my parents and other adults around me whenever I heard them discuss politics. I used to listen to the radio and heard Hitler's shrill harangues. Little by little, I picked up what the political parties were all about.

There was tremendous social agitation and huge political rallies. Everyone anticipated a major event, because the economic situation was so desperate. My parents talked about politics endlessly — it seemed they never talked about anything else.

Before the elections that gained the Nazi Party the largest number of seats, we thought that Hitler would never win. We believed there would be too much opposition to him, that the other parties would block his moves.

In fact, just the opposite happened. The right-wing and centre-leaning nationalist parties regarded the Communist Party as their main opposition. Many people, at least in our area, expected the Communists to win. So, following the elections in July and November of 1932, when both the Nazi Party and the Communist Party attracted strong support, Hitler skillfully used fear of communism to swing the moderate parties behind him. By manipulating the Red Scare, Hitler managed to attain power with support from the moderates.

I remember my father's prognostications: "If Hitler gains power, he won't last more than six months. Hitler doesn't know economics. He can't run Germany without knowing economics. He can't run a complex government in a modern society."

The election returns were close. In our region the Nazi Party wasn't strong, but that didn't make any difference. After a series of weak short-lived governments, Hitler was asked to become chancellor at the end of January 1933. My parents were stunned; they couldn't imagine what the next step would be. They knew Hitler's political and social philosophy but didn't take him seriously: my father described him as an adventurer who couldn't hold things together. He thought the economy would collapse under Hitler.

My father misjudged Hitler completely, as did many others inside and outside Germany. People deluded themselves: they thought Hitler could be controlled, or they brushed him off as a temporary aberration that would soon disappear. And they were so mournfully wrong. Hitler dominated everyone around him. Using surprise, propaganda and violently repressive tactics, he lasted much longer and did indescribably more harm than was ever predicted.

Within a year of taking office, Hitler had eliminated all the other political parties. Germany became a one-party state. Hitler forced everyone to fall in line or risk severe penalties or death.

Shortly after the Nazi Party assumed power, my uncle Josef was savagely beaten. The skin across much of his body turned blue with terrible bruising. The assailants warned him to clear out of Bochum.

A foreign newspaper printed a picture of him to illustrate Nazi brutality. My uncle was a bellwether in 1933, a sign of what was to come. He owned a fashionable shoe store in nearby Bochum that was favourably located and always crowded with customers whenever I was there. It was a gold mine, according to my father.

He was hospitalized for two weeks. When he was discharged, he came to our house to hide. Since his picture had been published abroad, he was afraid of being beaten again or killed. For six weeks he hid in a small room in our attic, terrified of being found and too scared to return to Bochum.

We never knew why he was attacked. My parents immediately assumed that it was a personal attack and not an assault against Jews — such was their faith in German civilization. I now think that his business success had aroused poisonous envy and made him an early victim. He was certainly not a communist; on the contrary, he was an outright capitalist.

Around that same time, the principal of the *Freie Schule* in Wattenscheid, an admirable man called Rector Mank, who was a true democrat and a pacifist, was summarily exiled by the Nazis to a one-room school in a remote part of Germany. Rumours of other attacks and demotions circulated, and many reports of these appeared in the newspapers abroad. But Uncle Josef was the only Jew we knew to whom this sort of thing had happened. My parents shrugged it off. "This isn't the end of the world," they said. "Maybe he did some harm to someone, and that person took revenge."

But after that, Uncle Josef was afraid to stay in Germany. He sold his business and moved to Palestine. There were no currency restrictions yet, so he took all the money he had with him. He left Germany with his family in 1933.

Unemployment went down swiftly after Hitler rose to power. He built armaments and prepared for war. The economy recovered in a phenomenal way. Our stores were crowded from morning till evening; we could barely handle the volume.

The next disturbing incidents took place at my *Gymnasium*. Students began joining the Hitler Youth. Soon they were wearing the uniform — brown shirt, black pants and big belt — to school. Teachers also joined the Nazi Party. The Nazi Party anthem, *Horst-Wessel-Lied*, and other songs associated with the Nazis were sung at class meetings. I was also the only Jewish boy in my class and eventually I was the only one in the class who didn't belong to the Hitler Youth.

The odd thing is that, even though they belonged to the Hitler Youth, many classmates were still my friends. Most of them didn't stop talking to me. It was like the Boy Scouts at first — simply a club they joined that I didn't. All of them knew I was Jewish, yet they didn't ostracize me. In the early years, I felt only slight discomfort. But the strain increased inexorably as time went on.

⁓

Before 1933, there was little cohesion among Jews in Wattenscheid. My father, for one, had a low opinion of the services at the local synagogue. Every year on the High Holidays, on Rosh Hashanah and Yom Kippur, our family used to walk to and from the synagogue in Gelsenkirchen, four kilometres each way.

After 1933, though, the Jewish community in Wattenscheid began to come together. Since Jews were excluded from clubs and activities, we created our own groups and social events. A varied and active community life developed for those few remaining years. Every Friday night and Saturday, for Shabbat, all the young people flocked to the synagogue. When my brothers and I got involved, our parents were drawn in too. My father joined us regularly, even though he had seldom gone to synagogue before. He wasn't a religious man, but he came with us because he felt he should.

It was remarkable to see all the Jews in synagogue. We never lacked a minyan or quorum; until then, such participation had been impossible. People drew together as the larger community pushed them out. Now synagogue became the centre of our lives.

Wattenscheid was too small to have a rabbi of its own. Instead, we had a cantor who also acted as rabbi and gave sermons, but whose main occupation was as a teacher in the *Freie Schule*. Cantor Oppenheim had been my class teacher in 1932, my final year there, and his brilliant daughter, a professor of linguistics who had a doctorate in pedagogy and had specialized in English, had been our first English tutor.

Long established though small, the synagogue was furnished with simple benches. Women sat in the balcony, and men on the main floor. A short distance away was the *Gemeindehaus*, the community centre, where Cantor Oppenheim lived in the rooms upstairs. Downstairs, there were meeting rooms and games rooms, with Ping-Pong tables and chess, checkers and card tables. We organized frequent events and many Zionist activities. Every Saturday afternoon, we held an Oneg Shabbat, a sabbath celebration, where Cantor Oppenheim told rabbinic stories and we sang Hebrew songs.

The cantor trained all the young men to daven, to pray. He taught us to read the Torah with *neginot*, the proper liturgical chant and traditional melodies. He instructed us in how to perform as the *chazzan*, cantor, ourselves and how to lead prayers. He gave us repeated opportunities to practise. On Friday evenings and Saturday mornings and even on holidays, the young boys had the honour of assisting him, taking over parts of the service.

Cantor Oppenheim was a typical German schoolmaster. He had high standards and paid great attention to detail: every phrase had to be exactly right. He wouldn't accept half-hearted attempts. I never forgot what he taught me and will always be grateful to him.

I continued bravely on at the *Gymnasium* in Wattenscheid, while my brothers were pupils at a Jewish school in Gelsenkirchen, which they went to by streetcar every day. My brothers and I were quite different. I was a bony child, and with my thatch of platinum-blond hair I was nicknamed *der Alte*, the old one, by my classmates. My serious demeanour and my years with Baba Shoshi had made it easy for me to sit for hours with adults. Benno was becoming a tall, athletic fellow with red hair, fair skin and large brown eyes. People often admired Benno's deep, dark eyes and Eddi's thick, wavy, black hair. When Benno was little, Eddi and I used to tease him because he was the youngest. As he grew older and more wiry, we backed off. He was excellent at sports and gymnastics. He became a better soccer player than Eddi, who was good at every sport.

Though I was keen about most athletics, my physical skills didn't match my enthusiasm, so my participation was limited. Besides, when I was twelve I began to wear glasses due to my near-sightedness. At first, I was ashamed of them and used to put them on only in class to see the board, but after a while I had to wear them even to play soccer, even though they risked falling off and breaking. So as time went on, I was usually found in the cheering section at soccer games.

My brothers and I, especially Benno and I, were soccer fanatics. Our favourite team was Schalke 04, which won the German championship several times during the 1930s. Another team we followed was SV Höntrop, whose stadium was within walking distance of our home. Benno and I spent many a Sunday afternoon at the games, often to the consternation of our parents. I knew the players' scores better than Benno did, but Benno knew them better than Eddi did. Eddi liked to do things rather than talk about them, whereas Benno compared records, discussed moves and also played well himself.

We all did well in school, but I felt increasingly uneasy at the local *Gymnasium*. The usual salutation between teachers and students had become "Heil Hitler," and even more Nazi songs were sung fervently at school assemblies. I knew it was only a matter of time before I'd be expelled or something worse would happen. So in 1935 I told my father I wanted to join my brothers at the Jewish school. My father tried to dissuade me, because the Jewish school was mostly a primary school with a few classes for the higher grades, not like a *Gymnasium*. Finally, he gave his consent.

However, my father was right, and soon after changing schools I told him that I would prefer a *Gymnasium* after all. After a few months, I quit the Jewish school and enrolled at the *Gymnasium* in Gelsenkirchen. Other Jewish boys from the area were there, and this lessened the pressure from Nazi sentiments and ideology.

In 1935, Germany was now openly re-arming, and many armaments were being produced in our region. Hitler began to urge the nation to protect itself in case of war by building bomb shelters, which the government would subsidize. Accordingly, my father applied for a subsidy and installed a shelter in our cellar. It was completely furnished and stocked with dried foods and other necessities. Living under extreme conditions was becoming imaginable, even palpable.

Some time that year a letter arrived from Australia, like a voice from another world. It was from a man named Rosen, who had emigrated. He offered to reciprocate my father's generosity: Rosen had toiled in the coal mines near us until my father had given him a start in business. He was now successful in Australia and was confident that my father would do well there too. He urged my father to let him help us secure immigration papers. The man's gratitude and the offer astonished my father; in fact, when I think about it now, it seems to me it truly alarmed him. Rosen Textile Mills, Sydney, Australia, was the return address on the envelopes I would handle wonderingly. My father's response was consistently negative; he claimed he knew very little about Australia. "Where's Australia? What's in Australia?" he would mutter.

Then my father ordered us to stop discussing the subject. He refused to move and never considered the opportunity properly. I can hardly bear to think how he must have begun to regret this decision very soon afterwards.

Other people were leaving. In 1936, my bachelor uncle, Mischel, who lived in our house and managed our furniture store, decided to pack up and get out of Germany. He went to live in Palestine, where he died in the 1960s (it had by then become Israel). I never saw him again after he left Germany.

Later that year a fire broke out in our clothing store, and a section of it burned. My father was arrested and accused of setting the fire — highly improbable since sales were booming!

Erwin Schrock, a master tailor working for my parents, was also living over our store. He and his wife, Hedwig, occupied the apartment next to ours. Hedwig had been a nursemaid in our home at the age of sixteen, in 1923, before Eddi was born.

Hedwig and Erwin had virtually become a part of our family. They lived in the annex of our home because my parents wanted them nearby. Both my parents were deeply attached to the Schrocks, and the Schrocks were devoted to them. Baba Shoshi and Uncle Mischel had both been very fond of golden-haired Hedwig, whose Slavic face regularly burst into radiant smiles; my mother, an only child, treated Hedwig like a beloved younger sister. Similarly, my father and Erwin were like brothers.

Erwin came from Stettin in the province of Pomerania, a part of Germany (now known as Szczecin, Poland). In 1921, when he was twenty-two, he began to work for my father and stayed with him from then on. Erwin was capable, good-looking and elegant. He was also an intelligent, independent-minded man. My father trusted him completely and relied on him increasingly in business matters.

After our store burned and my father was arrested, Erwin checked around the building. He found matches that had evidently been left by whoever had set the fire. He showed these to the police; they then arrested him, too, and charged him with being involved!

My father was kept in the prison near Wattenscheid for four weeks; Erwin was held for two weeks. He testified unsuccessfully as a witness in my father's defence.

Because German newspapers were severely censored by the authorities, we began buying Swiss German-language papers from Bern and Zurich. In those newspapers, we read articles about Dachau. The camp, opened in 1933 in a suburb of Munich, was the first concentration camp created by Hitler. Jews and non-Jews, communists, socialists and others who opposed Hitler's policies were being thrown into Dachau. People were suffering and dying there because of mistreatment, malnutrition and slave labour. This was all well known at the time; my parents talked about it at home.

Knowing this, we were relieved my father wasn't sent to a concentration camp. He was kept in an ordinary jail and underwent the usual prison treatment. Then he and Erwin were released, and the whole matter seemed to be put to rest. None of us talked about it afterwards.

After this episode, the day's receipts from the stores were kept by Erwin. My father had begun to realize that we were losing our rights, yet he was determined not to be intimidated into leaving Germany. My parents often discussed the possibility of leaving. My father, however, felt there was no reason for him to have to leave; he would go on his own terms or not at all. Losing his property, let alone his life, was not in his plans.

By 1935–36, it was becoming clearer to him that all might not turn out well. But we were prosperous, and when people are living affluently in the country of their choice or birth, they don't readily detach themselves from it.

More significantly, my father was forty-two years old in 1936. For a man of that age with numerous attachments and dependents, emigration is a serious decision. Exile isn't an option that a responsible person chooses lightly.

From late 1935 on, my parents' plan was to send their children away, starting with me. After that they would see what happened. They thought they had some time, not expecting events to occur as quickly as they did.

I continued at the *Gymnasium* in Gelsenkirchen until the spring of 1937. I had just completed the German school system's *Obersekunda-Reife*, which was similar to a junior matriculation or intermediate high school diploma. In another two years I could have sat for the

Abitur or senior matriculation, but I couldn't continue there any longer. It was almost impossible by that point for a Jewish youth to attend a German *Gymnasium*; the pressures were becoming overwhelming. The Hitler Youth had by then been indoctrinated for several years. To hate Jews was their supreme mitzvah, their first commandment. One of their major tenets held that Jews were the cause of their *Unglück*, their misfortune.

Many young Nazis had a mystical feeling about Germany and about having a mission to fulfill. A main aim of this mission was to wipe out all the Jews in Germany. Jews were classified as rats, sewer rats, vermin. Hitler and his propagandists inveighed against Jews constantly. The evidence of this mountain of propaganda is still there for all to see in the press and posters of the time; the world had never seen its like, a truly modern weapon in ideological warfare.

Schoolmates were baiting me and sneering, "There's no place for you here. Why don't you go to the Holy Land? Why don't you get out of here? We have no use for you. You're responsible for all our troubles." They would become frenzied. It wasn't possible for me to study among them or to be among them.

Hamburg and Cologne — which was closest to us — each had a Jewish *Gymnasium* that covered only the intermediate level. In Frankfurt and Berlin, Jewish *Gymnasia* offered the higher grades.

I told my father that I could no longer attend a public *Gymnasium*, that I couldn't stand it. Eddi had gone to Berlin the year before, after he graduated from the Jewish school in Gelsenkirchen. In Berlin, he was attending an ORT school, a trade school for Jewish boys run by the Organization for Rehabilitation through Training. My father suggested that I join Eddi in Berlin. As a result, I applied and was accepted at the Adath Israel *Gymnasium* in Berlin. I was fifteen years old. It was time for a change.

Departures

My father accompanied me to Berlin to help me settle in. Eddi moved out from the family he'd been boarding with, and together we moved into a kosher hotel on the Kurfürstendamm. By then Eddi knew his way around the city, so I was quickly oriented as well. Berlin was overwhelming, but at the same time the anonymity of the big city was a relief in its own way.

I began studying at the Adath Israel *Gymnasium* in April 1937. I found the standards very high, and it took me weeks of strenuous effort before I caught up to the other students — they were better trained than I was in the basics. At the school in Gelsenkirchen I had been easily the best student; the school in Berlin, however, admitted only top students from all over Germany. Many of the teachers, moreover, had taught in German universities but had recently been forced out; they were far more scholarly than the high school teachers in Gelsenkirchen.

The school comprised a few hundred boys, with thirty-five or forty to a classroom. I was in the *Unterprima*, the next-to-final class. It was a stimulating environment and an exacting one.

Some boys in my class were preparing to write the Cambridge English exam, which could be written in Germany even then. If they achieved high scores, they had a chance to gain admission to Cambridge or Oxford. I knew several students from the *Gymnasium* who accomplished this. In due course my father suggested to me, "Why don't you take the exam? Maybe you could study in England." My parents were always proud of my scholastic ability and had lofty aspirations for me. I began, with direction from my teachers, to drill myself to write the Cambridge exam.

For social life in Berlin, Eddi and I joined a Zionist group, a youth branch of the Mizrachi organization called Brith Hanoar, to which we had already belonged at home. An active unit flourished in Gelsenkirchen, and I had been the secretary and had met touring national leaders there. Since the leaders we had met there were mainly from Berlin, Eddi and I resumed acquaintance with them now.

Some of these youthful Zionists became prominent in Israel later on. Many founded kibbutzim and some served in the government. I remember Yosef Burg of Leipzig, who became a long-time cabinet minister in Israel and was a vigorous Zionist organizer when I was in Berlin.

Another person I remember who attended Adath Israel *Gymnasium* concurrently with me was Walter Wurzburger, who hailed from Munich. He went on to become one of the most distinguished Orthodox rabbis in North America.

Among students at the *Gymnasium*, the major issue concerning us was passing our exams. I'd been more concerned with the state of Germany while in Gelsenkirchen and Wattenscheid than I was in Berlin. The population was diverse and cosmopolitan and there were many Jews. Eddi and I felt safer than we had in a small town where we could be pointed out as one of the only Jews. In Berlin, I concentrated on passing the next exam and paid little attention to politics.

It was an insular life. My parents weren't around me constantly talking about politics with friends and anyone else who dropped by. My brother and I were living among transient strangers and we spoke about politics with no one. We scarcely read newspapers or listened to the radio because there seemed to be no point, as both newspapers and radio were under complete government control. We became less involved in political events even though we were closer to so many of them.

While we were in Berlin in 1938, our uncle Beryl, his wife and youngest son, whose home was in Oberhausen not far from Bochum, were expelled to Poland. From there, by a circuitous route they made their way to Palestine, where the two older sons had gone a few years earlier. Now our immediate family was the only one left in Germany. All our close relatives had gone. My father's mother was still in Poland, and his sister, Gusta Schmidt, was in the Netherlands with her family. Everyone else had left Europe.

~

On November 7, 1938, a junior official in the German embassy in Paris whose name was Ernst vom Rath was shot. His assailant was a teenage Jewish boy. In retaliation for this assassination, the Nazis proceeded to destroy Jewish property and levy taxes on German Jews.

Kristallnacht, the Night of Broken Glass, started on the ninth day of November. That night and into the following night, squads of Nazis invaded Jewish neighbourhoods. They smashed windows. They looted and set fire to Jewish homes, factories, stores and synagogues.

These depredations struck many small towns, as well as Berlin. In small towns all the Jewish real estate was targeted and blighted. But Berlin was a huge metropolis, and so it was possible to not see Nazis' violence and destruction. Eddi and I still lived on Kurfürstendamm, which was and still is one of the main avenues. It was a mixed area, not especially Jewish. Our district was undisturbed, so my brother and I were unaware of what was happening around Germany.

We got up to go to school on the morning of November 10, 1938, as we did any other day. Suddenly the telephone rang with a call from our mother. The time was seven o'clock. She blurted out that my father had just been arrested again. She was alone and didn't know what to do. I was so shocked at the news of my father that I don't even remember if she mentioned what had happened to the store. She told us to come home immediately, even though Eddi and I might have been safer in Berlin.

After her call, we hurried home by express train. We arrived in Wattenscheid, reached our gutted store, greeted our haggard mother and sat down to drink tea in the kitchen. The police turned up soon after and arrested Eddi and me right there.

We were flung into the jail in Wattenscheid. That night we were transferred to Herne, about twenty kilometres away. Our Aunt Rosa, my father's sister, had lived in Herne with her husband and children until they left Germany in the early 1930s.

We were detained in the jail in Herne along with other Jewish boys. One was Walter Nussbaum, whose home, like ours, was in a nearby town. We got to know him quickly in those unusual circumstances. Many years later my brother would find him again in Israel. And he still maintained his sense of humour: once he said to my grandson, who was on a visit to Israel, "You know where I met your grandfather? In jail!"

Locked up in Herne, I kept wondering where my father was. Then a talkative police officer revealed that we were supposed to be shipped to the Sachsenhausen concentration camp, but the camp was full. He said, "You're lucky, you guys. You're sitting here in Herne, not in Sachsenhausen like the others, the ones ahead of you." My father had been seized ahead of us, so I surmised he was in that concentration camp, located near Berlin. The Nazis were still somewhat deterred by the effects of overcrowding; years later, overcrowding in the camp wouldn't have entered into their considerations.

After two weeks, my brother was released because he was only fifteen. I was held for four weeks, because I was already sixteen and regarded as grown up. I suppose they were hoping to find room for me in a camp with adults.

My mother had been unrelenting in finding a way to free me. She had even managed to obtain an exit visa for me to leave the country on a Kindertransport. Several countries, such as the Netherlands,

England and Denmark, agreed to accept a fixed number of Jewish children from Germany. Thanks to my mother's efforts, I was scheduled to be part of one of those transports. Unluckily, I was slated for the Netherlands instead of England, which would have been much safer.

The last day I was in Wattenscheid, my father returned home. I learned then that he had indeed been in Sachsenhausen, one of the worst concentration camps in that period. He looked weak; he had been ill and hadn't yet recovered.

He called me aside and said to me, "You're leaving today, and I may never see you again. I want to tell you something," pausing, "I'm not supposed to tell you this," he confided. "I had to swear I wouldn't mention it to anyone. If it's discovered that I have spoken about this, I may be arrested again. But I'll tell you anyway."

He went on. "When I got to Sachsenhausen, the first thing I had to do was stand in line with other men for twenty-four hours. We weren't allowed to go to the toilet. If any of us became unsteady or fell, no one helped him. Anyone who fainted was shot on the spot and carted away."

My father had been in the army; he had endured severe conditions in the war. He continued, "There weren't many of us who stood still for that long. Those who did were assigned to barracks and put to work. We had to move heavy rocks all day. We loaded them onto wheelbarrows, pushed them from one place to another and dumped them out. Then we had to reload the wheelbarrows and move the rocks back! Meaningless work! All day long, every day. The guards hit us, beat us and gave us very little to eat. It was inhuman. Many people died."

My father was a strong, robust man, but he fell sick in Sachsenhausen and was put in the camp hospital. After four weeks in the camp, he and others arrested on Kristallnacht were released. Maybe the Nazis freed some individuals to warn Jews to leave Germany, to drive Jews away so there would be no need to deal with us further.

My father was lucky to be free, but he reasoned that they wouldn't let him go the next time.

He had opened my eyes to the terror of Sachsenhausen. "Remember," he drummed into my ears, "whatever you do, never enter a concentration camp. Never put your foot in a concentration camp."

He gave me this extraordinary message, the most important instruction I ever received. He directed me to do everything I could to stay out of a concentration camp. "Because once you're there," he warned, "you'll never get out. It's torture."

He made clear to me what the Nazis were doing in the camps. They debased and weakened people; abuse, starvation and excessive labour were just some of the ways the Nazis were murdering the Jewish people.

With that message, my father told me all I needed to know about the concentration camps. Until then I hadn't realized what these places were really like. We had heard about Dachau: we knew that some Jews and Roma and nonconformists were imprisoned there. But arrests had been on a relatively small scale.

Suddenly, we were all candidates for the camps. The Nazis' camps took on a whole new meaning.

My father galvanized me with his warning in December 1938. It was the last time I saw my father and the last day I saw my mother and my youngest brother, Benno. I never forgot my father's message. I never allowed myself to be deluded. His words were always uppermost in my mind throughout the horror of the coming years.

My father was too spent to see me off, but my mother and brothers escorted me to the station in Gelsenkirchen. There I boarded the train that took me across the frontier into the Netherlands.

~

All I had was the small suitcase we were allowed to bring, along with ten Reichsmarks, which was all the currency we were allowed to take out of Germany. My mother had supplemented this with a piece of jewellery, a fine gold chain set with a jewel, which I hid deep in my jacket. That was all I took with me: some clothing, ten Reichsmarks and a bracelet.

The train was the ordinary one that ran between Gelsenkirchen and the Dutch border. Jewish children occupied several railway cars. The Gestapo officers who climbed aboard to check our papers, even though each of us had a special visa, were rough and insulting to us.

My train went only as far as the Netherlands. Other trains carried children to England and elsewhere. It was just by chance that some children went here, others there; little forethought determined the destinations. Faced with the choice of letting me rot in jail or bailing me out with a guarantee that I would leave Germany, my mother had snatched at the first refuge offered, and that was to send me to the Netherlands.

In the evening I crossed into the Netherlands at Winterswijk, but at the border I was interned immediately as an enemy alien! I had been a prisoner in Germany and no sooner did I touch ground in the Netherlands than I was imprisoned again. It wasn't as bad as the German jail, but it wasn't the warm welcome I had hoped for, either.

The institutions involved with refugee children were the Dutch government, local churches and Jewish organizations. The first thing the Dutch authorities did was load us on a bus. We were driven to a village called De Steeg, near Arnhem and not far from the German border. There we were taken to a building that housed children in the summer, which was empty in the winter. The location was pastoral and pleasant, overlooking the IJssel River, a tributary of the Rhine. However, the beds in the dormitory were small; they were designed for young children, but we were adolescents. The Dutch had expected a transport of little children. They weren't prepared for us and had to make use of whatever quarters they had. They were now undecided about what to do with us.

I was in De Steeg for a couple of weeks before being shifted to naval quarantine barracks in Rotterdam. I was interned there like a criminal.

I was feeling lonely and unwanted, so I wrote to my aunt Gusta, my father's sister who lived in Maastricht, and she came by train to visit me. It took her the entire day to get to Rotterdam and then to the barracks where I was being kept. She brought a large basket of fruit and chocolates and talked with me for a while. She described the red tape she'd encountered at the gate of the naval installation before she was allowed to see me. But I was so glad she'd persisted — that little bit of family warmth meant a lot.

From Rotterdam I was transferred again, this time to a youth hostel near the city of Deventer. It was still winter, and the hostel, a recently constructed building, was only occupied in summer. Its facilities were just right for us, but we couldn't stay there long. With summer approaching, youth hostellers were expected, and we would have to move again.

We were given no regular schooling and had to find ways to pass the time. I had lost the opportunity to write the Cambridge exam, but I tried to continue learning something, anything. I studied Italian and a few other things on my own. Classes started, but they weren't well organized. We lacked essential texts and were never in one place long enough to make any headway. I now needed to always wear my eyeglasses, maybe because of the stress I was under, though I hardly let myself acknowledge these feelings.

Occasionally, we had visits from Jews who lived in Deventer. One was a man who travelled on business to Maastricht, which was about two hundred kilometres away. He offered to take me with him so I could visit my aunt. I was given permission to go with him twice. The route we followed paralleled the Dutch-German border, and Dutch police, who appeared to be on high alert, stopped us several times to check our papers. In Maastricht, the man left me with my relatives for a few hours while he attended to business. We would return to Deventer that same night. These excursions were a blessed change from the monotony of internment.

I tried to learn to garden in the spring in Deventer — I was bursting to learn something or do something. There was a trade school in the town, and after repeated attempts I succeeded in getting my name on the list to learn plumbing, which seemed to be a useful skill. Before I could start apprenticing, I was moved again.

We were taken to an abandoned orphanage in Gouda, the city famous for its cheese. The orphanage was an antiquated building in the centre of the city. Dilapidated and dirty, it was a thoroughly unsanitary place. In the dormitories, the beds were set close together, and outdoors we were packed into a small courtyard. Once again, we had nothing to fill our time.

Diphtheria flared among us. Some became very sick, and all of us were infected. I never developed the disease, but I became a carrier. We were tested for diphtheria regularly, and anyone who tested positive was confined to hospital. I was eventually placed in quarantine in the hospital in Gouda.

I wanted to conceal the worry about this disease from my parents, so in my letters to them I pretended none of this was happening. In that period, however, each letter from a contagious-disease ward was fumigated and the edges of the envelopes were cut off. I wondered if my parents realized the situation I was in.

In 1939, my parents struggled to find a way to leave Germany through official channels. By then Jews were forbidden to withdraw money from the country, so my father shipped a room-sized container full of valuable precision tools and small machinery addressed to relatives in Palestine, thinking he and my mother and my brother Benno might follow. The shipment reached Italy and went no further; there it went astray. The British aggravated the critical situation by blocking entry into Palestine. But no other country would accept Jews, so of course people thought more and more about getting to Palestine.

My aunt Gusta tried to pluck my family out of Germany in 1939 by sending a car with a Dutch driver to pick them up. But my father insisted on having authorization to leave. Stubbornly, he cited his

German citizenship and military service; he refused to sneak away from Germany.

Maybe he could no longer see things for the way they really were after the experience in the concentration camp. Maybe his mind could no longer take in what was happening. Or maybe he simply gave up, lost his gusto. I phoned them sometimes, and they could phone me; the short distance between us made this possible. I still had some hope, though it was slowly diminishing. There was no way they could legally leave Germany now.

In May 1939, my brother Eddi went to England on a Kindertransport, and Benno could have gone with him, but my mother wouldn't let Benno go. "I'll be alone," she wrote. "There'll be no one at home. I can't let all three of you go." She seemed so bereft that Benno told her he didn't want to go. My poor mother.

In September 1939, the war broke out when Germany invaded Poland. I was still in quarantine in the hospital in Gouda. A nurse who showed compassion for us said to me one morning, "War broke out today," and then brought me a newspaper.

Shortly after that I received a letter from my parents. They told me they had moved from Wattenscheid to Dortmund. I learned that the Jews in Wattenscheid had first been forced to move into the town's *Gemeindehaus*, where they had stayed until they were taken to Dortmund.

The move disturbed me and filled me with dread. I told the nurse, "This is the last time I'll ever hear from them. This is the end." She tried, nonetheless, to console me. "Don't say that. You never know," she said. But I was very close to correct.

Much later on I learned that after Eddi and I had left home Nazis would loiter outside our stores. They badgered the Schrocks with remarks like, "Did the Jews rake in money today?" They threatened to blow up the stores. They harassed Hedwig and called her "Jew wife" because of her friendship with Jews.

Then one day trucks drove up, and Nazis removed all the goods from our stores. My parents and Benno were ordered to live in a small room behind the Schrocks' apartment. They were forbidden to work from then on. Someone was appointed by the Nazis to administer our property. So much of the whole Nazi fabrication came down to property — it always did.

Later that year, because I was only a carrier of diphtheria and wasn't sick, the Dutch officials decided it was too expensive to keep me in hospital. I was transferred to the harbour area of Amsterdam to a quarantine station normally used by seamen. The barracks and huts were very old. I stayed there in isolation for a couple months with nothing to do.

Having been a member of Brith Hanoar, I established contact with the group in Amsterdam. Members of the organization came to all the detention centres looking for volunteers to prepare to go to Palestine. The group operated two kibbutzim in the Netherlands, one near Amsterdam and one in the northern province of Friesland. I volunteered to join one of these, to go on *hachshara*, the preparation and training for collective farm life. I was accepted into the hachshara in Franeker, a tiny city to the north.

But first I had to be cleared of diphtheria germs. There was no penicillin or other antibiotics at that time; my own body had to destroy the infection. I was kept with other infected people, so even if I overcame the disease I could be re-infected. My body eventually developed some immunity.

I had to sign a plethora of documents, but I was finally granted temporary residence and a work permit. This meant I was being released from custody, and in December 1939 I was suddenly a free person, exactly a year after I had left Germany. I had spent a whole year in the Netherlands doing absolutely nothing, except contracting a contagion due to poor conditions — the overcrowding, inadequate food and substandard housing. I still had a German passport with a swastika on the cover and a large "J" for *Jude*, Jew, stamped inside. But I now had Dutch resident status. I was accepted; I was legal. I could walk in the open air. I could breathe. I had nothing but my papers, yet I felt wonderful.

~

I had now joined the hachshara in Franeker, about twenty kilometres west of Leeuwarden, the capital city of Friesland, and a short way from Harlingen. This was an isolated region of the Netherlands, with its own marked dialect and its own distinctive character. The land is very flat and close to the sea, a windy, lonely landscape.

Friesland is rich farming country with excellent farmers. These hard-working farmers were grim and taciturn, barely speaking under any circumstances. One of the few remarks they made to me regularly was a proverb on the weather. It went:

Morgenrood
Brengt water in de sloot.

The proverb says that if the sky is red in the morning, it's going to rain (there will be water in the ditch).

Conditions were difficult for the Friesian farmers. They rose at four in the morning and worked steadily until six in the evening, labouring almost without pause. It was quite the preparation for a city boy like me.

We were a group of about twenty-five young people, fifteen boys and ten girls. Most of the girls worked in the houses, though a few were apprentice gardeners learning from a horticulturist. The boys worked on farms. The leaders of our organization demanded that we train hard, grow tough and learn to be skilled farmers from the Friesians.

We all lived together in a former train station in Franeker. The tracks had been removed, and so the place had been vacant until our arrival. Our organization adapted the building for our use: the ticket office became the kitchen, and the waiting room a boys' dormitory, while the girls slept in a room upstairs. We each had our essential bicycle, which we stored in a shed beside the house.

At 3:30 in the morning each day, we sallied forth on our bicycles. We were required to be on the farms by four o'clock, when the farmers began milking. There was a main road with bicycle paths, as there are all over the Netherlands to this day, where I could pedal safely. However, to get to my destination I had to turn off this path and struggle for five to ten kilometres along narrow, rutted back roads flanked by wide ditches. In that part of Europe, farm buildings are placed far out in the fields. It often snowed, and back roads in particular weren't cleared of snow early in the morning. I couldn't tell where the road was under the snow and where the ditch started — I landed in an icy ditch almost every day.

Country life was completely new to me; the closest I had ever come was my idyllic childhood summer in Galicia, in Poland. It was especially difficult because I had just emerged from quarantine, having done nothing for a whole year, and I had never before had to work physically hard. In Germany, I had just been a student, chiefly of language and classics, growing up in one of the most technically advanced regions of Europe and in the cosmopolitan city of Berlin. Suddenly, I had been thrown into a grind of hard physical labour with people who seldom talked to me. When they did speak, I couldn't understand what they were saying, since they spoke Friesian and I only knew some Dutch. Over the previous year as I was interned, I had learned a little of the language, since it was the one thing I could learn there. But these Friesians spoke their own dialect, which was very different from standard Dutch. They had no respect for me and always called me *Jood*, Jew, never using my name. They were very narrow-minded people who weren't at all accustomed to strangers.

They even disliked other Dutch people. And we were Jews, urban Jews. They didn't know what to make of us: they seemed to think we were demons or some other weird creatures. They accepted our presence because we worked for them for a pittance. They had dirt-cheap labour, and we had our training.

It was difficult to gain the Friesians' confidence, but once we did, they became somewhat friendlier toward us. They were not really willing to teach us much, though this varied with each farmer: some were more patient than others. The one I worked with first was a youngish man. I wasn't the strongest fellow around, and he continually discouraged me. "You'll never learn how to milk," he droned. "You'll never become a farmer. You'll never learn it. You're wasting your time." I was unhappy and asked myself, "What am I doing here? I'll never be a farmer! I'm working my heart out for nothing."

I hated my difficult early morning travels, tumbling into a ditch every time. The whole endeavour was ridiculous, and I was sorry I had undertaken the training. But I had no alternative, since if I had quit, I would have been interned again. I was only set free to work on the hachshara.

We were expected to spend about a year on one farm before being allowed to rotate to a new farm; we had to establish our tenacity. Many Jews at that time believed that persistence alone proved a person's value. An ideological glorification of labour had affected us. Zionist groups exalted manual labour, reversing the centuries-old trend of Jews as merchants and scholars.

I was lucky to have a few warm-hearted friends. One of them was a rabbi, Yehoshua Wolf. He had been a rabbi in Berlin, and I remembered hearing of him there. I was eighteen years old, the youngest on the kibbutz, and Rabbi Wolf must have been about thirty. He gave *shiurim*, or lessons, and I was a very good student; he liked me because I was the most intellectual in the group.

Yehoshua Wolf was a man with two left hands. He couldn't do any of the manual work even passably well, so he spent his time studying. As a result, he was ridiculed by some of our members, but I respected him. To me he was a learned man with a great reservoir of knowledge.

Another close friend on the kibbutz was Aaron Rath, who was also from Berlin. He'd attended the university there, but he was also skilled at manual work. He told me often to just keep at it, stick to it, and I'd be a farmer as well as a scholar. Every day Rath said, "I'm going to measure your shoulders now." Then he'd take out his measuring tape and stretch it across my back.

"You see?" he'd exult. "Your shoulders are already broader than they were yesterday! You get stronger when you work." What he said was true. "Every day you get stronger. I saw it myself," he'd say as he displayed his muscles. He always made me feel better. "Work! Work! Don't take any notice of what the farmer says." He'd clown and play little tricks to encourage me and cheer me up.

A shortage of nutritious food was a serious problem on the kibbutz. We ate only kosher meat and received provisions from Amsterdam every week. However, we never had enough to satisfy the appetites of young people employed in heavy labour, and I was hungry much of the time. But no doubt about it, I was getting tougher. Things were actually starting to look up a bit.

The hachshara had existed for several years before we joined it and included both refugees and Dutch citizens when I was there. Since half the members were Dutch, it wasn't like a refugee camp. A number of individuals had already gone to Palestine from the hachshara, and some members had already been training for a year or more by the time I joined. The Dutch Jews were much more at ease than the rest of us. They understood the language and could pick up the dialect well. They felt at home. They often helped us out, speaking to the farmers on our behalf.

I encountered my distant cousin Moishe Heller in Franeker. Like Rabbi Wolf, he was ten or twelve years my senior. The Hellers had lived in Hanover in Germany; I knew of them from my parents, but I had never met any of them. When I discovered that Moishe Heller was related to my mother, he took some interest in me. He too encouraged me and helped me to persevere. "You know, it's tough for all of us," he said. He had been in Franeker for some time and was considerably fitter than I was. He had already switched to his second farmer, one more likable than mine.

They were mainly dairy farmers in Friesland. On the first farm where I worked, my principal job was milking cows. Milking may look easy but it's not, believe me. I had to learn the proper technique and develop the right muscles, but I finally got it despite my complaints.

The prospect of simply reaching the farm each day was discouraging, nevertheless. The farm was so far from where we lived, and pedalling there in the winter conditions continued to be a battle against wind and snow. After milking the cows at four in the morning, I would feed the animals and clean the stable. I then prepared more fodder and attended to other chores. In the early afternoon, I repeated the same routine of milking, feeding and cleaning. In warmer weather, in between the stable chores I worked in the fields haying or spreading manure. I was busy until six in the evening, with only one or two hours of rest during the day.

I was relegated to the stable and never entered the farmer's house. A typical Friesian farmhouse was very large: the small front part, which had a tiled roof, was the farmer's home. The large back section had a thatched roof and contained a barn and a high hayloft. I was strictly a farmhand and never even saw the kitchen or the inside of the house. Even the other farmhands were contemptuous of me at first because they couldn't figure out who or what I was, though after a while some of us became friendly with each other. The farmers, however, never invited me into their homes. I never got anything from them, not even a kind word. Each day I brought my own bread and my own Thermos. I was paid four guilders (about two dollars) a week. It was a rough life — but at least it was a peaceful one.

Invasion

Every Friday afternoon our group stopped work early to go to the municipal baths. There we bathed, showered and donned our best clothes. Then we hurried to our house where we held our Friday evening service. We sang *zemirot*, songs, and I learned many new melodies. Some of these songs sounded strange to me, because they came from Sephardic Dutch Jews, but they were very beautiful.

Our Shabbat services on Friday evenings and Saturdays were very pleasant and informal. We were often joined by a Jewish psychiatrist from the psychiatric hospital in Franeker. When he was obligated to say Kaddish, the mourner's prayer for the dead, we congregated at his home on the Voorstraat in the centre of Franeker. Usually, though, we set up a chapel in the dining room of our house. The rabbi officiated and delivered a sermon: he gave lessons on the *sidra*, the Torah reading of the week.

On Sundays we resumed our work at four in the morning; we milked the cows early and again in the afternoon, but we were free in between. The people of Franeker and the surrounding area went to church, and so we did a half day's work on Sundays.

This routine continued smoothly throughout the winter of 1940 and into the spring. I grew stronger and coped with the work more easily as time went on.

We listened to the radio and heard rumours daily that Germany was planning to invade. No one believed it. The Netherlands had been neutral for a long time: the Dutch had stayed out of World War I and had often avoided the major European wars. There was no credible indication that the Germans would invade.

Then on May 10, 1940, it suddenly happened. I was at work on a farm when I heard the report. The farmer repeated an announcement he'd heard on the radio: the Germans were crossing the border. Troops were invading the Netherlands from multiple directions.

Without hesitation, I told the farmer, "I have to go back and talk to my colleagues." I felt we had to do something. I was not the only one in our group who had fled the Nazis, and now here they were, coming after us again. We knew they would repeat their past atrocities here.

I almost flew on my bicycle to the hachshara, arriving around ten o'clock in the morning. A few others had already returned, including my cousin Moishe Heller, whom I looked up to for advice and support. I spoke to him and the others, "Look, we have to get out of here fast, take our bikes and try to reach the other side of the Netherlands. Maybe we can board a boat to England. We have to clear out, otherwise we'll be trapped. We may never get away."

Moishe was opposed to the idea. He was a cautious man who tried to plan every move carefully. "Let's use our heads. Let's reason things out," he said. He thought I was panicking.

I said to him, "Don't pretend the Nazis use reason. They're not reasonable people." I knew their mentality. I had gone to school with the Hitler Youth. Their devotion to the Führer had reached such proportions that I believed they would go to extremes for him. My father's warning also echoed in my mind.

Most of the others in our group, especially the Dutch, were cool to my proposal. They didn't know what the Nazis were like.

A fellow from Bavaria, Benno Jacobs, was part of our group. Even through the thickness of his Dutch, I could detect his Bavarian accent. Benno and I wanted to escape from the German onrush. We decided to get on our bikes and pedal as far as we could in the direction of Amsterdam or Rotterdam. We would try to ship out from one of the harbours on the coast or from the Rotterdam area. We were the only ones who left. We took nothing with us — no food or change of clothing.

At about eleven o'clock that morning we hurried away, pedalling furiously. We intended to get out of Friesland, the northeast region of the country, and head down the western side. The entire country was gripped by confusion, and we had no information about what was happening.

From Harlingen we pedalled down the coast. About twenty kilometres from where we'd started, we came to a very long causeway that crossed the Zuiderzee, a body of water now called IJsselmeer, or Lake IJssel. We saw troops beside the causeway but paid no attention to them as we barrelled ahead.

The soldiers stopped us at the causeway and asked who we were, demanding to see our identification papers. We had no papers, since we had left them in Franeker.

The soldiers were stopping everyone, attempting to identify German invaders, including those who had parachuted in wearing disguises to blend in, with machine guns under their clothes. We found out later that paratroopers, masquerading in that fashion, had been part of the forces that would occupy Rotterdam.

We were arrested by the soldiers at the causeway, and our bicycles were confiscated. We were seated in a corner near the water with several soldiers standing guard over us.

We sat there for a few hours wondering what would be done with us. We tried to explain who we were, that we weren't German soldiers or spies; we were German refugees, Jewish refugees. We protested to our guards that we would never help the Germans conquer the Netherlands. But the Dutch soldiers were excited and on edge and ignored our explanations. They kept insisting that we were German spies.

There was mass shock and bewilderment that day, so we could hardly blame them for not believing us. The entire country was in turmoil. The Dutch hadn't fought a war in so long that they were completely unprepared, and the German attack had taken them by surprise.

After a few hours, we were ordered onto a bus that had arrived. The bus was then driven around in a zigzag course to numerous villages, picking people up. At first Benno and I were the only civilians on the bus, then other people were collared. We didn't know who was being picked up or why.

Suddenly, we heard German planes overhead: they started bombarding the road we were driving on. Machine-gun fire from the planes almost hit the bus. With a Dutch security vehicle tailing us and other soldiers guarding the bus and standing upright in the doorway, our bus surely looked like a military vehicle, too.

The planes flew on and gradually the bus filled up. We crossed the long causeway from Friesland into northwest Holland. We were again strafed on all sides. We drove on. Finally, we came to a city called Hoorn, north of Amsterdam — an old prison fortress surrounded by water. We stopped.

We were hustled off the bus and into a cellar deep inside the fortress, where we were locked in small, dark cells. We remained there for days with little food and saw nobody.

Benno and I were sharing a cell with several other men, but we never spoke to them. We couldn't see anyone clearly in the dark. We were wary of everyone, so we scarcely talked and barely slept. There were loud explosions nearby. We heard artillery fire and bombardments. At least we were safe from bombs deep in the fortress.

Then one morning we were all led upstairs. And who was there? German army officers! They shook hands with each one of us and congratulated us on having survived the bombing. Then they subjected us to speeches about the war and the German empire that had now been expanded. The Netherlands had now become part of the German empire, they said, and they were looking forward to our collaborating with them in assimilating the country and incorporating it into the thousand-year empire.

They spoke on and on as we were served hot coffee and food! We were ravaged with hunger.

We found out who our companions were: they were all Dutch Nazis and German infiltrators. We had been thrown in with them! The paradox of paradoxes was that, on the fifteenth of May, we were free men in the Netherlands and freed by the German army! The officers even offered us a lift to Amsterdam in a German army truck. We climbed on the truck, and a German army driver took us to Amsterdam. Two German Jews liberated in the Netherlands by the German army — it was rich, though we still didn't feel like laughing. Our identity was never even questioned by the Germans. They were on top of the world, and all was going according to their plan.

We arrived in Amsterdam to find it completely deserted, as everyone had gone into hiding or run away to the countryside. Benno and I roamed the streets looking for people who might help us, but we couldn't find anyone.

We went to the head office of our organization, which was also empty. When people eventually showed up there, they were mystified by our presence. When we told them what had happened, they gaped and shrugged their shoulders as though we had concocted the story. They just couldn't believe it.

We decided to return to Franeker, since there seemed to be nothing else to do. All transportation in the country had stopped, so we stayed in Amsterdam for six days until trains were moving again.

The Germans were now engrossed in military operations in Belgium and France; they weren't much interested, it seemed, in the civic setup in the Netherlands. Benno and I managed to get back to Franeker without incident and found all our colleagues still there. Nothing had happened to them.

⁓

I resumed my work on the farm as if nothing had happened. The summer was lovely that year. There was scarcely a sign of the military occupation — we seldom saw any Germans in our corner of Friesland. Once in a while, a patrol passed along the highway, which we could see from our house on the Harlingerweg, the road to Harlingen. Motorcycles with sidecars would clatter down the road infrequently, and the Germans neither stopped nor talked to us. The summer was a quiet one.

I transferred to another farm at the end of the season. Moishe Heller had worked there and recommended the place to me, since it was easier work than what I had been doing and more diversified. The new farm was north of Harlingen at Sexbierum, close to the sea, which was much farther away from where we lived. This was the only drawback, as it took me more than an hour to get there. Fall and winter wore on, and I often had to cycle straight into stiff sea winds.

Still, I liked working there because I learned more than just how to milk cows. Plowing and field work with horses and growing potatoes were all part of the job. The farmer was a specialist in growing potatoes. The production of seed potatoes was a major industry in Friesland. Friesians grew some of the best potatoes anywhere, many for export. There wasn't much trade at the time because of the war, but normally their potatoes were shipped all over the world.

I was very impressed with the way the potato industry was organized. Every few weeks an inspector would come into the field. He scrutinized every plot and assigned them each a grade: A, B or C. If the plants were tall and dark green with no sign of disease, the potato plot was given a high grade. The better the grade, the higher the selling price, so farmers worked hard for the top grades and good returns.

The Dutch also established courses in milking, and milkers had to pass examinations. The farmers paid workers according to the grades they achieved on these tests. The farming industry in the Netherlands was extremely well operated.

Besides working and learning how to farm, I took all the courses in religion offered by Rabbi Wolf in the evenings. We studied Mishnah, the oral common law, and Gemara, debates on the common law, as well as Jewish history. Every Shabbat we discussed the Torah portion of the week. Rabbi Wolf was a gifted teacher, and because of his association with us, I had a rare opportunity to learn.

There was a furniture factory where many carpenters worked next to the old train station where we lived. I was now well into my gruelling second year as a farm labourer and I really wanted to acquire a trade or profession other than farming, so I talked to some of the factory staff, who were ready to take me on as an apprentice. I proposed this to our group, arguing that in the Land of Israel carpenters would be needed as well as farmers, since all kinds of skills are required to build a country. Our leaders brought my request to the highest council in Amsterdam, who decided to reject my request. I was told that the reason for the decision was that the organization wanted all of us to know how to farm.

Our group did, however, notice my talent in discussing religion, and they eventually decided that the group might benefit from sending me to rabbinical seminary in Amsterdam to study for a year — not to undertake a full degree, but to learn enough so the group would have a second person who could direct religious studies. Rabbi Wolf sponsored me strongly for this. He contended that we needed young people trained to lead discussions, interpret the Torah and teach others. The leaders in Amsterdam voted in favour of my coming to Amsterdam for a year to study at the seminary.

In September of 1941, for Rosh Hashanah and Yom Kippur, the High Holidays, I visited my aunt Gusta and her family. I had stayed in contact with her since she had visited me in Rotterdam when I had first arrived in the Netherlands and had since spent many holidays with her family. Aunt Gusta was devoted to me because she had lived with my father when she first emigrated from Poland. She had kept house for him when he was struggling to build up his business and felt very close to him. She tried to do whatever she could to make me feel comfortable in her home. Now and then, she also sent me money by mail. She always said my father had sent it for me by courier, but by that time I rarely got any notes or letters from home, so I don't know if this was true. She may have been giving me money of her own.

Aunt Gusta was strikingly good-looking, with black hair, dark brown eyes and clear skin. Her features were small and neat, characteristic of our family. She was slender and graceful, with a riveting presence that drew people to her. She was also unusually kind and generous, genuinely good, radiating the same benevolence as my father. He was an open-handed man who would empty his pockets for someone in need without expecting thanks, and Aunt Gusta was exactly the same. She had tremendous warmth and humanity. Whenever I visited her in Maastricht, she treated me like a prince. I never had such treatment from anyone else.

Aunt Gusta and Uncle Shalom had five children, three boys and two girls. One had the unusual name of Schneewittchen, which is German for Snow White. The boys were my age and a year or two younger; we always had fun together. The family had been in the Netherlands since 1933 or 1934. When they had lived in Germany, they had barely scraped by, but in Maastricht they had done well. Uncle Shalom, a devout and humourless man, owned a furniture store and seemed more than adequately successful.

Visiting Aunt Gusta's home was my holiday from hard labour. To get from Franeker, close to the most northern point of the Netherlands, to Maastricht, near the most southern point, I had to cut right across the country, a trip that took a full day by train. There were German soldiers guarding the stations, but they were not interfering with the daily life of civilians, as far as I could see. And so I made my way to my aunt's house without incident.

The food was traditional and always plentiful: baked carp, chicken noodle soup, roast chicken or boiled beef, potato pancakes, red cabbage and sponge cake. Her meals were much more satisfying than those on the hachshara, where we lived on bread, milk and boiled vegetables, mainly potatoes, peas or beans. Doing farm labour and eating little meat is a debilitating combination, and it was a struggle to constantly work hard when our diet lacked sufficient protein. Under the German occupation, it was particularly difficult to get kosher meat to the tiny community of Franeker; in Maastricht, kosher meat was still readily available.

During that holiday visit, my aunt and uncle were concerned about the German occupation. I met several other Jews from Maastricht at their home. No visible action had been taken against anyone, but the ominous mood was overwhelming.

Back on the hachshara after the holidays, in October 1941, our group was called to meet with the Gestapo in Leeuwarden and to bring our visas and passports. The Gestapo examined our papers and asked us questions before letting us go. Prior to this, we had had to report a few times to the small police station in Franeker.

On the hachshara we foolishly believed that we would be able to leave the Netherlands, that somehow the Nazis would let us go. In Germany they had permitted emigration until late in 1939. But then the British blocked immigration to Palestine, and with a war going on there was now no longer any way to even travel to Palestine — no passenger ships, no civilian traffic. It had become almost impossible to get there.

As the war escalated, the chances of fleeing from the Netherlands were approaching zero. No other country would provide asylum. The Germans closed the borders, stopping all exodus.

The Nazis had established the Joodse Raad, Dutch for Jewish Council, in the Netherlands, but nobody knew its intended purpose. Rumours began to circulate that the Jewish Council was "recruiting." At first it was young people between the ages of twenty and thirty who signed on for work camps, and the rumour was that they would work for the Germans in war industries. Way up in Franeker, we were never part of that recruitment.

I was no longer able to phone my parents. I think long distance calls were being restricted to military business. I wrote letters to them, and they wrote to me; sometimes the letters got through. My parents' letters were always short, since they were under surveillance and letters were censored. But I read between the few lines and understood that they weren't doing well. I worried about how they were living from day to day, how well they were eating, how their health and their spirits were holding up, what treatment they were being subjected to.

All the Jews in the Ruhr Valley, including my parents, had by now been rounded up and herded into segregated Jewish houses in Dortmund, where they were confined. In the Jewish house, my parents and Benno had two rooms, a bedroom and sitting room, in a house with many other Jews. Jewish-owned businesses were all closed. My parents were not allowed to work; they couldn't earn any money. They were living in Dortmund on the same street as some distant relatives. My youngest brother, Benno, was there supporting them, learning to be a carpenter by working in heavy construction for some entrepreneur — at least, that was what they told me. In 1941, Benno was just sixteen years old.

In the fall of 1941, I received a letter from Eddi through the International Red Cross. I was astonished to see it came from Canada! Until then I had thought Eddi was in England, because I had not heard from him since he had gone there in 1939. He wrote, however, that he had been interned in England because he was a German citizen and had then been shipped from England to Canada along with other German Jews and German prisoners of war. Now he was in an internment camp near a place called Fredericton in New Brunswick, working in the forest felling trees. He'd had to use a Red Cross form letter, without much space to write, but receiving even that thin lifeline to my brother was a wonderful event. I could only think how glad I was that he was well — and well away from Europe.

I was still on the hachshara. I had recently begun working on a farm very close to where we lived, which meant I was even able to go home for breakfast. This farm was one of our group's preferred placements because, being on the Harlingerweg just beyond the psychiatric hospital, it was about three minutes from our old train station by bicycle. No more worrying about falling into ditches in the early morning! It was also a clean place to work, and the owner was fair-minded. I inherited the job from a colleague because I'd become an excellent milker. The farmer Van der Berg had a large herd of cows, so the job required an experienced hand.

I was working out in the fields one cloudy day in late 1941, in the cool, rainy weather we often had in Friesland. By then the solid manure that had been collected all year had grown into a bulky pile. Liquid manure had also accumulated in the ground in large containers that were cemented and covered, so that later it could be sprayed on the land with hoses attached to special carts. That autumn morning, we were trucking solid manure out to the fields. A crew was loading the manure onto two or three carts, which operated in tandem; when the first cart was full, a farmhand drove it to the field, unloaded the manure and came back for the second load. I was driving a cart pulled by two horses. Suddenly, when I was out in the field with a load, the horses shied, then went wild. The cart, manure, horses and I flew into a ditch. I could have been killed if the cart or horses had fallen on me. Miraculously, I landed on top and slowly sank into freezing water.

When I failed to return for a while, the farmer grew suspicious. He came after me and found me near the ditch. I had scrambled out, and the horses had also got out; the wagon was partly smashed. The farmer tried to retrieve whatever he could, before telling me to go home, change my clothes, get a hot drink and keep warm. He saw that I was shivering and feeling a bit sick.

So I went home and changed my clothes. I drank hot tea and got into bed to warm up. It was about eleven in the morning. I fell asleep.

At about two o'clock, I woke up. I heard boots, German boots, marching onto the former station platform in front of our house. A small army was assembling there. I thought, *This is it. They've come to pick us up.* We'd been wondering why they had never bothered us.

I pulled the blankets over my head and played dead. The room was large, the main waiting room for the train station, with twelve or more beds in it, some of them bunk beds. When they spotted me, one of the officers, in typical Nazi fashion, raised his foot and shoved me with his boot. Then he kicked me. Finally, he ordered me in German to get up immediately.

The others stalked the room and tore it apart, combing through everything. They opened cupboards and knocked things out. We had little in them, but anything we did have was thrown to the floor. Beds were overturned.

Then the officer said to me, "You line up with the others." Some of the soldiers went upstairs to the room where we stored a few bags of food and cans of vegetables. Soon these soldiers came out screeching, "See what these Jews are hoarding? They're hoarding food!" We had barely enough to eat for the next day; there was absolutely nothing to hoard. We had a few bags of beans and potatoes. "Hoarding and hoarding and hoarding!"

They lined us up on the platform. We stood there for a couple of hours. They were waiting for everyone to return from work. They were rounding us up to take us away.

The Dutch police were there too and were helping the Germans by describing the region to them and informing them where all our members worked. They went as far as to fetch some back themselves, rounding up quite a few of our members. I was struck then by the close cooperation between the Dutch police in Franeker and the Germans.

I was standing in line, still jittery from my tumble into the ditch that morning. German soldiers were posted all around. In desperation, I spoke in German to a soldier and said, "Look, I have almost nothing on. Can I go inside and get my jacket? Can I go and get my jacket?"

He answered, "No. No. What do you need a jacket for? You won't need a jacket where you're going."

I asked him again. In spite of what he'd said, he seemed to have a little sympathy, especially when he heard me speak in German. And sure enough, this time he grumbled, "All right, go ahead. And come back fast." The Nazis were always ordering everyone to do everything *schnell*, fast. So I did.

I scurried into the station house. The place was a wreck. Instead of looking for my jacket, I raced to the back door. The back door of the station house was blocked by a heavy case, but I thought if I could move it aside and open the door, I might get away.

Even weak people can sometimes summon unusual strength when it's really needed. My hair was short, unlike Samson in the Bible, but I had more of it then than I have today. And like sightless, enfeebled Samson, I exerted enough force to move that case.

I immediately opened the door and without even looking left or right simply threw myself out. With one jump, I landed in the ditch behind the station house.

The guards had noticed nothing. A guard stood at each end of the back of the building, but they were facing the front, not expecting anything to happen at the back. I listened for a moment, waiting for reactions, and then I crept along the ditch. The ditch was filled with tall grasses and water, slowing my movement. I knew that in two hundred metres or so I would reach an open field. If I kept my head down and moved quickly and carefully, I might get away.

I reached the field, then a row of houses nearby. A farm worker acquaintance lived there. I knew the Germans would be looking for me as soon as the soldier who had let me go noticed my absence. I saw an empty kennel with no dog in sight and quickly decided to hide in it. I crept inside and crouched low. It was roomy, for a kennel!

I stayed there until dark, then decided to move. I thought I might find one or two of my friends and try to save them; I hoped they weren't all rounded up. One fellow, Bram, always returned late in the evening because he worked on a distant farm. I headed in that direction.

Under cover of darkness, I ventured down the road and was lucky enough to intercept him. Bram was a Dutch Jew, a big, brawny fellow, who had had less difficulty with the local people than I had. On the farm where he worked, he'd become close friends with a Friesian who owned a little farm of his own. We decided to go to this farmhand and try to hide in his barn for a while.

We went to Bram's friend and explained why we had come. We persuaded him to go to Franeker that night to find out what was going on. He knew everyone in town, and he dropped in at a local bar and talked to people gathered there. The day's event was the most exciting thing to hit Franeker in years, and the town was buzzing because of it. Townsfolk said all the Jews had been rounded up except two: one had escaped and the other couldn't be found. The Germans were looking for both of them. The other Jews were now in prison in Leeuwarden. The Germans had ransacked the old station house.

Bram and I hid out on his friend's farm for two days. We knew the Germans were hunting for us.

However, we also knew we had to abandon the area. Although the Friesian farmhand backed us a hundred per cent and would have concealed us indefinitely, there was no reason for us to stay there with everything we were linked to destroyed. More importantly, since Dutch police were collaborating with the Gestapo, we had very little chance in such a small community of not being caught eventually. By hiding us, the farmhand was also running a great risk, since at some point someone would have betrayed him.

We decided that on the third day at five or six in the morning we would try to take the first bus out of the neighbourhood. From a station further south, we would take a train to Amsterdam.

Our plan succeeded. We got away from the farm and left the area on a bus from a village near Franeker. We first went to a small city called Sneek. We saw German guards at the train station there but passed them without being questioned. Our pictures weren't in circulation, so they couldn't easily identify us. Contrary to common Nazi belief, the Germans couldn't actually easily identify someone as Jewish. We boarded a train to Amsterdam that afternoon.

When we arrived in Amsterdam, we felt obligated to report to our headquarters. The officials sent us to the Joodse Raad, which occupied the same building. Our organization respected the purpose of the council.

We presented ourselves at the council office, and the functionary in charge exclaimed, "Oh! You two are here! We've been waiting for you. We've been looking for you."

I said, "What do you mean, looking for us?"

"I just had a telephone call," he answered, "from the chief rabbi of Leeuwarden. The Gestapo have been in contact with him. They told him that unless you two report voluntarily and give yourselves up, all the others will be shipped to Westerbork." An internment camp established by the Dutch in the late 1930s, Westerbork had become a German camp.

I hissed at him, "I'll tell you something. They have twenty-five of us now. If we give ourselves up, they'll have twenty-seven. All that you will achieve is sending two more Jews to Westerbork."

"Shame! Shame!" he cried. "It's your duty to stand with your colleagues, to stand side by side with your comrades! Don't you have any feeling of responsibility?"

I shouted back at him, "My responsibility is to save myself! Bram's responsibility is to save himself! Along with anyone else we can help. But we can't save the others! I know the Gestapo. It's certainly not my responsibility to cooperate with them! By giving ourselves up, we'll achieve nothing, nothing! We would just be helping the Nazis in their filthy work!" I knew this immediately, though I couldn't convince this pompous creature, who was either deliberately harmful or a dupe and a fool.

I'm glad to be able to record that our organization supported us completely after this interaction. Bram and I split up, and our officials arranged for me to spend a few days with a Sephardic family by the name of Rodrigues. Distinguished people who were deeply religious members of the renowned Portuguese Synagogue of Amsterdam, they were very kind and concerned. Since I couldn't stay with them long, they found another place for me.

I moved to the Koster house. The Kosters were Jews who lived in the Zuid, south, a wealthy enclave of Amsterdam. Their mansion commanded a sheltered street of imposing homes off a wide boulevard called Apollolaan.

Koster was the most eminent professor of accountancy in the Netherlands, and also directed a private firm. Many top students of accountancy in the entire country came to study with him.

The Kosters had four children, one of whom had a cognitive disability. The family had had severe problems with that child and employed a specially trained nurse solely to care for him. My arrival on the premises was the result of their need for a maid. Their house soared several storeys high and contained many spacious rooms and bathrooms, and so I became a domestic in the Koster house, as they needed somebody to do the heavy work of scrubbing floors, cleaning carpets and washing windows. By then Jews were no longer allowed to hire any non-Jewish help. Semicloistered, I couldn't ramble outdoors at will; my rights had disappeared, and my name was on the Gestapo's wanted list.

False Identities

I devised a new strategy to correspond with my parents. I wrote to my parents as usual, but I signed my name as Eli Hart. Eli Hart was a member of our group in Amsterdam, a Dutch Jew who lived beside one of the canals there, the Herengracht.

I explained nothing to my parents about what had happened; they understood. It must have caused them some worry, yet they never questioned the change. Because I signed my letters Eli Hart, they simply started to address me by that name. And Eli brought me the letters that came to him from my parents. It was November 1941 and Moritz (Moishe) Schnitzer didn't exist anymore.

So began my false identities. Even though it was no longer safe to use my own name publicly, the Germans weren't putting a lot of effort into looking for me, since had they tried they could have traced a connection from Schnitzer in Germany to Eli Hart and me in Amsterdam. They had other priorities.

I worked in the Koster house from November 1941, my status slightly higher than that of a maid. It wasn't a pleasant life, but neither was it really unbearable. There was always enough to eat because the Kosters were rich. They bought food on the black market; there was never any shortage.

When I moved to the Koster house, I no longer saw Bram. Although his family lived in Amsterdam, he dropped out of sight.

Another member of our hachshara named Menachem (Piefke) Levy had been in Amsterdam when the Gestapo rounded up our group. He had been on a visit for several weeks, having stayed in Amsterdam to recover after falling sick during his trip. But now his name was also on the Gestapo list.

Piefke was about a year older than I was. Extremely religious, he had belonged to the Agudath Israel movement, an Orthodox religious group. He came from Hamburg, Germany, and had studied at the Jewish *Gymnasium* there.

After I moved to the Koster house, I looked for Piefke. I thought he was likely living close by and found he was only three blocks away. He was staying with wealthy, prominent Jews who lived in Amsterdam Zuid. They had nurtured him back to health and treated him like their own son. He was not working in their house.

For months, my only recreation was to visit Piefke. In the evening I sneaked over to where he was staying. We talked and played chess, as there wasn't much else we could do. I couldn't move about openly: it was dangerous for me even to answer the doorbell because the Gestapo might appear at any time to search the Koster house.

I had been living and working at the Koster house for several months when, in April 1942, the Nazis made it mandatory for every Jew in the Netherlands to wear a yellow star. I reasoned that, since I was already wanted by the Gestapo, why wear a yellow star? So I decided not to wear it and never did. This in itself was a dangerous breach of the law, but I believed that it was wiser for me to violate it than observe it.

The Kosters were taking a big risk by harbouring me; Koster was a man inclined to take chances. He often travelled to The Hague and Rotterdam on business, and he never wore the yellow star. He boasted to me, "You don't wear a yellow star — I don't wear it either!" I admonished him, saying, "You have more to lose than I do. I have nothing to lose. I'm all alone. No one knows me. People recognize you. You're well-known. You have a family. You're a man of substance.

Why do you gamble like this?" He was exposing himself to arrest every moment.

The situation was getting worse everywhere. That same April, I received a postcard from Dortmund written by my mother and partly by my father. They wrote: "We're leaving for the east. We're leaving to work in the east." The message was obscure. "We're leaving now." It was a brief note in which they said that they and my brother Benno were going to a work camp and I should take care of myself. That was all. It was addressed to Eli Hart.

That was the last mail I ever received from my parents. It was the last time I ever heard from them. April 1942. A card with a few lines that conveyed an awful message.

Piefke's fiancée also disappeared at about this time. Rachel was from Vienna and had been with us on hachshara. She had been caught with the others and sent to Westerbork.

In May 1942, she was allowed to leave Westerbork for a visit to Amsterdam, which was very unusual. She stayed with Piefke for a week at the home of the family in Amsterdam Zuid, and I saw her there a few times.

Rachel was employed in sewing at the camp in Westerbork but talked very little about it. One condition of her leave may have been to keep silent about the camp; perhaps she had sworn, as my father had, to tell no one about camp life. But I could guess roughly what Westerbork was like.

I urged Rachel repeatedly to stay with us. I said to her, "Rachel, don't go back to Westerbork. We'll never see you again if you do." In the strongest way I could, I begged her not to go back. But she always replied, "I have to go back. I promised I would." I told her, "Forget your promise. Don't go back. Stay here. Don't go back or you'll never return." Yet when the week was up, she went back. I never saw her again.

I sometimes went out to try to buy vegetables for the Koster family. Shortages had become acute, and there wasn't much for sale except radish leaves. People were making use of greens that would normally be thrown away.

There were a number of markets near us. Suddenly, the Germans began to sweep through them. Amsterdam became a hunting ground. *Razzia* after *razzia*, raid after raid, took place. The Germans would storm a market and arrest everyone who was wearing the yellow star, shoving them into a police truck and hauling them away. I escaped several times simply because I didn't wear the yellow star.

Piefke and I decided then that we wouldn't survive in Amsterdam Zuid much longer. It was becoming risky for all Jews, even the Dutch-born and resident aliens who had legal visas and permits.

After the third or fourth raid, at the beginning of July 1942, we moved out of Amsterdam Zuid. I moved away from the Koster house, and Piefke left his place. We moved in with a family living near the Amstel River in the centre of Amsterdam.

In that district, too, raids were occurring frequently. One day the Gestapo burst into our house, and we sprinted to the top of the tall, narrow building and hid ourselves in between the rafters. We escaped detection by sheer luck.

We realized then that we couldn't stay in Amsterdam any longer. The option of emigrating to Palestine didn't exist anymore — we couldn't get out of Fortress Europe. Switzerland, Spain and Sweden were the only countries we could escape to. And so we resolved to make a run for Switzerland, since it was the only safe place we thought we could reach. We considered Spain, but concluded it was too far away and would probably involve crossing the Pyrenees Mountains. Access to Switzerland would be easier. We would travel south from the Netherlands to Belgium and France, then east to the Swiss border.

Piefke had an uncle living on the outskirts of Brussels. We decided to visit him first, gauge the situation around Brussels, and then elaborate our plans from there.

Before we left Amsterdam, I wanted to go to Maastricht to say goodbye to the Schmidts. I set out without the yellow star or a permit to travel. When I arrived at my aunt's house, she was overjoyed to see me. Uncle Shalom was hunched in the kitchen praying; he was reading *Tehillim,* Psalms. When he saw me, my uncle choked, "What are you doing here?" He knew I was on the run and that it was a crime to give me refuge. He asked shrilly, "You came here, endangering my family, my children, my wife and me?"

I answered, "Uncle, I'm not staying long. I just came to see my aunt. I want to say goodbye. I'm going to try to make my way out of the Netherlands."

Then I thought that maybe I could do something for the two oldest boys. I asked my aunt to allow her two oldest boys to come with me. I talked to them, too, and tried to persuade them to join me.

Their father reacted very strongly. "Who are you to tell the boys to gamble like that, to throw their lives away?"

I countered, "If we don't stand up for ourselves, who will stand up for us? 'Im ein ani li mi li?'" (If I am not for myself, who will be for me?) "God helps those who help themselves."

"Oh," he preached back at me, "the will of God will be done one way or another. If God wants us to live, we'll live; if He wants us to die, we'll die. Everything is in the hands of God."

Then he ordered me, "Out of my house this minute; get out of my house! Don't come back with your crazy ideas — talking to people about doing stupid things, especially my sons."

My aunt wept. She handed me some money, and I left. That was the last time I saw any of the Schmidts.

I returned to Piefke in Amsterdam. Together we collected some road maps and railway charts of the Netherlands, Belgium and France, mostly the kind used by students and hostellers. Then, still early in July 1942, we bought tickets for Beek, a town in the southern region of the Netherlands, close to Maastricht and the Belgian border.

When our train reached Beek, there were German soldiers on duty in the station randomly checking travellers, but they didn't stop us. We walked from Beek toward the Belgian border. Our maps weren't precise enough to tell us where the German garrisons were. The Netherlands and Belgium were both occupied by the Germans, so the line between them wasn't fixed at the time. Dutch and Belgian police controlled a few border points, but the border didn't really exist according to the Germans who passed back and forth without formalities.

As we crossed the border that evening, some tricky moments transpired when the Belgian police grew suspicious of us, but we managed to worm our way through and enter Belgium and made our way to the city of Hasselt.

From Hasselt we rode on a series of inter-city streetcars to Brussels. The next day we arrived at Piefke's uncle's home. His uncle was well off and lived in a villa in a quiet suburb of Brussels. We met several of his neighbours and friends, including a fine Austrian couple; the man was a Jew, but his wife wasn't. They'd escaped from Austria in 1938 when the Germans overran it and were living in the centre of Brussels near the famous little fountain called the Manneken Pis.

We stayed with Piefke's uncle while he helped us acquire important documents. We bought Belgian identification cards through a contact he had in the underground. Each card cost three thousand Belgian francs. My picture was attached to my card and then the official stamp of a Belgian town was impressed on it.

I had to give myself a Belgian name. Because of my passion for soccer and since the Belgian and German national teams played against each other every year or two, I knew of an outstanding fullback on the Belgian team by the name of Jan Van Capelle. So I christened myself Jan Van Capelle, the only Belgian name I knew.

I filled in the card myself. I invented the address Chaussée de Bruxelles (Brussels Road), reasoning that every Belgian city must have a road leading to and from the capital Brussels and designated so. The card was stamped with the authentic seal of Wavre, a city south of Brussels in the Belgian province of Walloon Brabant. The city was chosen for me, probably because a member of the Belgian underground worked in the city hall of Wavre or had a contact there with access to official stamps.

Like me, Piefke invented a Belgian name and address for his new card, which also bore the seal of Wavre.

Both Piefke and I had brought our *tefillin*, phylacteries, with us — we weren't thinking very clearly when we left the Netherlands! We were so devout that we put on phylacteries every morning to recite our prayers and never even thought of discarding them. We carried these small, square objects with us wherever we went. I always had mine in my pocket.

In Brussels, Piefke and I realized that we might step into some thorny situations on our way to Switzerland. It wouldn't be wise to have phylacteries found on us: they would give us away immediately as Jews. It was imprudent to have even taken them with us from Amsterdam.

Piefke's uncle refused to store the phylacteries for us, since he didn't want them in his house and didn't expect to stay in Brussels much longer himself. Instead, we left them with some non-Jewish neighbours of his, a respected doctor and his wife.

After this, Piefke and I set off to cross the border into France. We travelled first to the Belgian city called Tournai, which was across the border from Lille, a major city in the industrial area of northern France. Many Belgians living in Tournai worked in French industries and would pour into the area in the morning and stream back home at night. We learned in Brussels that large groups of people crossed the border every day at specific times, especially between seven and eight o'clock in the morning. We were told that we could cross into France there without difficulty, since Germans weren't stationed at that point because it meant little to them even though they controlled that part of France, too.

Piefke and I mingled with the crowd of people in Tournai and managed to cross the border with them without being questioned. We were relieved to arrive in Lille and strolled around the city. We began to prepare our next move, which was to try to board a train for the city of Nancy.

At the railway station in Lille, we were stopped by the Germans. They asked to see our papers. They were checking routinely for irregularities in documents and trying to find resistance fighters.

They looked at my identity card and let me go, but Piefke was arrested. Suddenly, I was alone. I didn't know what to do. I thought, *I've lost my companion! Here I am in Lille and I don't know anybody. I'm all by myself. I don't know what to do!*

I decided to move on — I had to keep going. I dragged myself onto the train and rode until the first stop, a town called Denain. I got off the train and asked for a room at a hotel near the station and spent the night there. The next morning, I was still mulling over the situation. I was shocked, disoriented; I couldn't collect my thoughts.

One train a day covered the distance from Lille to Nancy. I spent the day and another night in Denain and by morning had decided to continue on my way. The first person I saw on the train from Lille was Piefke! I looked up and stared at his face.

I had found him again; we had found each other. Somehow, he had talked himself out of detention. I was indescribably happy to see him. The two of us continued our journey and arrived in Nancy in the evening.

Nancy is a large city. We wandered from the train station toward a business district and, by chance, stumbled on a synagogue close to the station. German soldiers and Gestapo were passing by the building almost casually.

Piefke and I entered the synagogue and joined the men at evening prayers. The rabbi was elderly and dignified, and the men attending the prayers were formal and patrician. The Jewish community of Nancy dated back several hundred years.

When the service ended, the men huddled together talking privately in small groups. They sauntered outdoors to the courtyard. We joined them thinking they might help us, but they ignored us.

Then we noticed that we were the only ones not wearing the yellow star. Our accents, even in Hebrew prayers, were unmistakably German. Meanwhile, German soldiers and Gestapo were parading on the street nearby with a clear view into the courtyard, so these French Jews must have been bewildered by us. They probably worried about who we were and why we were there. And for two people bent on hiding our Jewishness, we had certainly strolled through the wrong door! We exposed our Jewish identity just by being there. German patrols marching by could have seized us at any moment.

Piefke and I glanced at each other apprehensively and quietly left the courtyard. We slipped into the back streets of Nancy, skirting the main parks and squares, and lost ourselves in the city.

It was growing late, and we were hungry. We couldn't buy food, since it was rationed and sold only with food tickets. We had no ration tickets.

We happened upon a system then that we used frequently afterwards. We entered the cathedral in Nancy and found our way to the confession booths. Piefke sat in one, I in another. We told the priest, "Nous sommes des juifs, mon ami et moi. Nous sommes des réfugiés en provenance des Pays-Bas. Nous avons besoin d'aide. Pouvez-vous, voulez-vous nous aider? Nous voulons entrer en Suisse. Pouvez-vous nous aider?" (We are Jews, my pal and I. We are refugees from the Netherlands. We need help. Can you, will you help us? We want to get to Switzerland. Will you help us?)

Piefke or I would say words like these in many churches, as asking for help in churches became one of our main survival techniques. It always brought us at least a meal.

The priest in Nancy was a young man, very sympathetic to us. He offered us a meal of bread and cheese, then advised us to travel via Besançon and to visit the archbishop there. He would help us with further directions. Besançon is close to the border, with many possible routes branching out to Switzerland.

So we pressed on from Nancy. There were few trains we could take, since the schedules had shrunk and the trains operating were full of German soldiers. It was hard to find a seat or even to get on a train, but we eventually managed to get on one. We moved on toward Belfort where we had to change trains. Luck, alertness and caution each played a part in our reaching Belfort and beyond, because the station was packed with Germans. Our hearts pounding, we plowed on, arriving in Besançon a day or two later.

Once there, we followed the priest's advice, making our way through narrow, ancient streets to the cathedral. The archbishop's palace stood opposite. We rang the bell at the gate, and an old woman came out to ask what we wanted. We told her that we had been sent to the archbishop by the priest in Nancy.

The archbishop received us in his office. We explained who we were and why we had come. He told us to sit down, then ordered his housekeeper to prepare a meal for us.

Since our aim was entry into Switzerland, we asked the archbishop if he had information about the conditions at the border. Besançon is approximately eighty kilometres from the Swiss border, but there was almost no official travel taking place at the time. No transportation system was operating between France and Switzerland, and the border was tightly sealed.

The archbishop gave us some specific directions. He told us to continue to a small town called Maîche near the Doubs River, which etches the border there between France and Switzerland. He recommended that we cross into Switzerland somewhere along that stretch of the river. After reaching the Swiss side, he advised that we head for a city named La Chaux-de-Fonds, in the Swiss canton of Neuchâtel, north of Lausanne.

A short time later, we started on a long trek from Besançon. We hiked through rocky meadows and pastureland and over forested hills. At one juncture, we met a group of people led by a guide and discovered they were Jews. We stuck close to them, following them, which vexed the group and guide no end. Hurling threats and insults at us, they tried to shake us off and finally succeeded.

In the rolling foothills of the Jura Mountains, the skyline of every village is dominated by a tall church tower or steeple; we moved forward from church to church. We were again fed by the priests and gathered information and directions from them. We advanced steadily this way.

Within a week, we arrived at Maîche. For almost two weeks, we scouted around the border at the Doubs River trying to find a safe way across. The border was heavily patrolled. We could see German sentries pacing with guard dogs on footpaths along the cliffs beside the river. The only food we ate was fruit we stole from trees on farms close to the border. Our stomachs ached with hunger. We hid and slept in the fields and woods. We moved around mainly at night, because movement was dangerous in daytime. The whole area was crawling with German patrols.

Switzerland was one of the few neutral countries in Western Europe. The German forces were on constant alert for spies and smugglers and other illegal traffic attempting to cross the border, making it one of the most heavily guarded borders in all of Europe.

On one of our scouting trips, we came to the top of a mountain on the French side. Perched above the river was an ancient village called Fournet-Blancheroche. In the village church, we found an old priest. When we told the priest that we were *juifs*, Jews, he cried out, "Vous êtes des anges, des anges." (You are angels, angels). He reacted as though he had never seen Jews before, as though we had stepped right out of the Bible.

He brought out a large bar of chocolate that he had been saving for a long time. I had never seen chocolate like it. He gave it to us, and we sat down to a wonderful treat. Then, demonstrating some worldly sense, he pointed out a house in the village and warned us that Germans were staying there. He described the route we should follow to find a safe place to cross the river.

Somehow, we lost our way. Perhaps his directions were wrong — sometimes our amateur guides didn't know the way well themselves — or maybe in our excitement we missed a turn. Whatever the reason, the path we took was full of patrols with police dogs.

It took us about half a day to work our way agonizingly down the mountainside, through the trees and underbrush, to the Doubs River. As much as possible, we tried not to slide down, so as not to tear our pants or ruin our clothes.

We had found ourselves at a spot in the Jura Mountains where the Doubs River runs through a steep but narrow gorge. The rocky bluffs covered with tall trees dropped abruptly to the water, but in spots a fringe of beach emerged beside the water, which we had made our way down to. The channel of the river along this strip was not very wide, but the water was deep and swift. On one side was France; on the other, Switzerland.

So we had finally reached the riverside, and no patrols were about. We could cross, but the river was wild, and I couldn't swim. Piefke jumped in and swam across. I thought maybe I would be able to swim, that maybe fear would force me to swim.

I jumped in the water, but I still couldn't swim and almost drowned. Clutching at some reeds, I managed to keep myself afloat and pull myself out of the water.

I was still on the French side. Piefke was already on the other side and called out to me. I thought, *Holy God, I'm going to be caught here.* The patrols would be coming by soon; I could hear the police dogs barking.

I scurried around and saw a boat chained to a metal stake on the bank. Could I tear the chain free or pull the stake out of the ground? Could I tear the boat loose? I had no tools, no equipment. I tore at the chain and pulled and tugged. I kept on pulling, tearing, straining. Almost anything is possible in extreme situations. I tore the stake out of the ground.

The boat was loose, but there were no oars in it. I jumped in and paddled with my hands. It was very awkward, and I could scarcely control the boat.

By sheer luck, I manoeuvred the boat into the middle of the river. At that point I stood up and heaved myself out. In one leap, I almost reached the other side. I scrambled to my feet and waded the rest of the way.

I was on the Swiss side and began to climb the slope. I had completely lost sight of Piefke. It was growing dark, and there were dense woods by the riverside.

I had barely made it to the Swiss side before I heard German voices on the other. They were shouting that the boat was gone, their patrol boat was gone. They hollered, "Wo ist das Boot? Das Ruderboot ist verschwunden. Etwas stimmt nicht." (Where's the boat? The rowboat is loose. Something's wrong.)

The dogs were barking fiercely — so fiercely, I thought they were going to cross the river. It was rumoured that German patrols sometimes crossed to the Swiss side to pick up whomever they were after, and that the Swiss weren't guarding the border diligently. I didn't see any Swiss guards at all, but the Germans didn't come across.

In the morning, I met Piefke high up on the hill. When we reached the top together, we lay down in the sun to dry our clothes, which were still soaked through.

We hugged and congratulated each other on our accomplishment. "We've done it! We're free! We're in a free country. We've put those miseries behind us."

We had succeeded beyond our wildest dreams. Together we had managed to enter Switzerland in late August 1942 without any money and without a guide. We had crossed three borders in about six weeks, a remarkable feat considering we had done everything more or less on our own.

Our next objective was La Chaux-de-Fonds, where we would search out the rabbi or some Jewish people to ask them to help us.

We resumed our journey. The region was full of trees and tangled undergrowth; our pants became torn and ragged from tramping through the bush. We reached an isolated farm and saw a farmer working his field. We spoke to him in French, asked him the way to La Chaux-de-Fonds and how far it was. He pointed to a road winding down the mountains and a small city far ahead in the valley. Then he said to us, "They're very strict with people who come across the border. They're arresting everyone. They don't want any refugees. I want nothing to do with you guys. I can't help you. You'd better get out of here. Go on. Go. And don't tell anyone you saw me."

We told him that we didn't want his help, we didn't want anything from him. We were surprised by what he had said. We thought the isolation had affected his brain or detached him from reality. We were sure he was exaggerating, that the Swiss would welcome us with open arms. Even if we were arrested, so what? We didn't mind being arrested by the Swiss; they wouldn't do us any serious harm.

It took us three days to reach La Chaux-de-Fonds after crossing the Doubs River. By that time, we were tattered, rumpled and dirty. We arrived in the small, attractive city of La Chaux-de-Fonds in the afternoon. Not knowing if any Jews were living there, the first thing I planned to do was find a telephone booth and look up Jewish names, like Cohen and Levy. We walked down the main avenue. Suddenly, a man in civilian clothes approached us and said, "Police suisse. Carte d'identité." (Swiss police. Your identity card).

It was three o'clock in the afternoon. The police officer arrested us and took us to the cantonal jail, which was so new and clean and warm that it seemed like paradise to us. We had been outdoors for weeks sleeping in forests and fields. We were put in a cell with two cots. Everything was neat and scrubbed.

At six o'clock, we were brought some food, consisting of hot black coffee and delicious bread. After living for so long off of stolen apples from trees, this simple food was excellent.

～

In the evening, at about eight o'clock, a police officer brought us to an office where there were other police, who began to interrogate us. The questioning went on for a couple of hours.

We weren't searched or told to empty our pockets. Although carrying Belgian identity cards, we didn't use them. We told the Swiss police that we were Jews from the Netherlands: Piefke and I had decided that it would be to our disadvantage if we said we were German Jews. We thought we'd have a better chance of being accepted into Switzerland as Dutch Jews.

We told them we had come all the way from the Netherlands, mostly on foot. We had crossed several borders, including the one into Switzerland. They wrote down everything we said. Then they went to the phone a few times, calling authorities in Bern to ask for instructions.

Eventually, at about ten o'clock, they told us, "There are too many Jews in Switzerland; we can't take any more. If we take any more, Switzerland will be overrun by Jews." They said, "If we let you stay, there'll soon be more Jews here than Swiss. It can't go on like this. We're very sorry, but you can't stay in Switzerland. You have to go back."

They had decided to expel us. This was the directive from Bern.

It was a terrible shock to us. After all our efforts to get there and the safety it meant to us, this decision was catastrophic.

The greatest insult of all was that we had to sign a statement declaring that we understood that if we ever set foot on Swiss soil again, we would be handed over to the Gestapo at the border. "This time," the Swiss police said, "we'll do you a favour. We'll bring you to the border at an unguarded point. We'll set you free. We'll let you run back across into France to try your luck somewhere else."

There were tears in Piefke's eyes. I didn't cry. I became very angry. I accused the police, "You're murderers. You've condemned us to death and you pretend it isn't so. We can't go back again; we had so much trouble getting here. You can't send us back."

It didn't upset them a bit to be called murderers, and their decision didn't change.

Then three or four brawny police officers walked in. They told us to stand up. They led us outside and pushed us into a car. Three of them climbed in with us.

It was after ten o'clock on a moonlit night. We drove to a clearing near a place called Le Locle. The car stopped and we were hustled out.

A police officer carrying two loaves of bread gave one to Piefke and one to me. Then he said to us, "This is the border. Go. In that direction. Keep on going, keep going. And never come back again."

Caught Between

The border was riddled with snares and traps. There was a Swiss zone, a neutral zone, then a German zone. We edged forward through these different zones. Suddenly, the Germans were shooting at us! We got separated as we dodged and tried to run for cover, and I lost Piefke. I don't know what happened to him and never saw him again.

The next morning, a farmer driving down the road on his wagon gave me a lift to a town called Morteau. From there, I took a train back to Besançon. I walked from the station down to the Doubs River, which winds through the city. Then I called on the archbishop again.

He recognized me at once. He said, "I know where you can smuggle yourself into zone libre" (Free Zone). The border between the two parts of France was not far from Besançon. "If you can get to zone libre, you could go on to Lyon. In Lyon, who knows what may happen?"

South of Besançon there is a town named Arbois. I was told I would have to cross a railway track to get to the border between the two regions. Many people crossed there, according to the archbishop, because the Germans weren't guarding as closely in that area. On a sunny afternoon at the end of August, I left Besançon by bus on my way to Arbois. Driving through rolling, hilly countryside covered with forests and fields, we passed through villages on the Doubs River. As we descended from the mountains into the valleys, a church steeple in the town was conspicuous in the distance. About two hours later, the bus arrived at the outskirts of Arbois. Grapevines covered the hillsides.

Then, startled, I noticed that the town was crowded with Germans. Arbois was virtually an encampment of the German army! Apparently, the Germans had just recently, perhaps even just that day it seemed, begun to plug the hole in the dam to stop the exodus of French people from *zone occupée* (Occupied Zone). The archbishop hadn't known about this development.

The bus stopped at the terminus. German soldiers were standing watching everyone who exited. I decided that I couldn't walk out the front door. Instead, I opened a window and jumped out the other side of the bus. I hurried away from the bus and disappeared from the depot as fast as I could.

I was in a dangerous position. The whole place was full of Germans, and they were patrolling the streets and squares and standing at every corner. It was impossible to avoid them.

I managed to slip into a church near the city hall in the centre of Arbois to talk to the priest. I said to him, "Can you help me? I have to cross over to the other side."

"Oh," he lamented, "vous êtes malchanceux, vous êtes malchanceux." (You're an unlucky one, you're an unlucky one). He continued, "You have come to the worst spot in France. You won't find a crack in that line now. The Germans have sealed it tight. There's no way to get across."

He gave me no hope and no help. He took me up to his rooms under the roof of a tall building behind the church and pointed down: "You see, that's the jail. It's full of refugees. They were all caught here." I looked down at a courtyard enclosed by high walls.

I had to flee from this area. I thought I'd be arrested right there — he was so terrified just having me there that I feared he'd turn me in himself.

I said to him, "Just tell me which way I should go?" He answered, "You see out that way? There is a railway track beyond there." He pointed toward the outskirts of the town; there was a railway station a bit of a distance away that we couldn't see from where we were, where a track ran behind, at the edge of open fields. There were hills and a forest beyond, in the near and far distance. He declared, "You have to cross that track to head toward the zone libre. Go that way."

I thought that it didn't look very far at all, perhaps several hundred metres away. German soldiers were patrolling the track. I would try to cross early in the morning, figuring that there wouldn't be many guards on duty then.

I skittered through the town toward the railway station and stole into a garden nearby. Sunflowers and other tall plants with large leaves were growing in the garden; I crouched among them and lay down to sleep.

During the night a violent storm blew up. The rain beat down. I tried to shield myself with flowers, but they didn't cover me. The leaves grew heavy with rain, drooped and dripped on me. Soon I was completely drenched.

I waited until daylight, then forced myself up. Hurrying from the garden, I made for the railway track. Suddenly, four uniformed Germans were blocking my way with police dogs. They arrested me. I acknowledged that I intended to go to the Free Zone, since I saw no point in denying it.

I did not really want to go to the Free Zone, because I sensed that it would not go well for me there, either. Maybe this feeling had come over me because the Swiss had driven me out, which I had never expected — I'd been thrown off balance. Then Piefke had vanished. After that, the archbishop and the priest had let me down. Worse still, I had made the same mistake in Arbois, walking around the town, that we'd made in Switzerland, walking into La Chaux-de-Fonds in daytime. I should have tried to leave Arbois during the storm at night.

I don't know why I didn't. Waiting until morning had been a serious mistake. After such blunders, shocking turns and misguidance, I could have lost the strength to survive.

~

I was put in the jail in Arbois. It was a small, old, dilapidated place. As the priest had said, there were lots of others already being held there. The German Geheime Feldpolizei, the Wehrmacht's secret military police, came and questioned me. That's when I invented my story.

I said I was Belgian and that the situation in Belgium was tough. I told them my parents were dead, but I had a brother living in Lyon. He had a business selling milk there and needed somebody to deliver it. I was on my way to Lyon to help my brother with his business.

That's what I told the German police. They sentenced me to three months in jail for attempting to cross the border. Three months in jail in Arbois. After that I would be sent back to Belgium to verify my identity card and confirm that I was who I said I was.

In jail in Arbois, lice were the biggest problem — the jail was swarming with them, the mattresses were full of them, and they spread everywhere. I had never had lice before, but I became infested like everyone else. I had lice in my hair and could feel them crawling on me. Whenever I touched my hair, I would pull out lice and crack them between my fingers. They pop as their body breaks. They were all over me, even in my armpits and pubic hair. I washed myself scrupulously, but the jail was so full of lice that I couldn't get rid of them.

My circumcision made me apprehensive, as well. Though other men were circumcised, too, not only Jews, I wanted to avoid any suspicion or questions about it, so I tried not to let anyone notice.

Some of the prisoners in the Arbois jail were criminals, but everyone there had been arrested for trying to cross into the Free Zone. When my three-month sentence was over, I started my journey back to Belgium.

The transfer was done in stages. I was first sent to Besançon. In Besançon, there's a vast and formidable *maison d'arrêt*, a prison situated on a butte above the old city. It's a classic prison with cell blocks radiating from a central tower and high walls surrounding the complex. Some wings were used by the French; others were partitioned for use by the Germans. Prisoner transports were assembled there.

I spent three weeks in solitary confinement in Besançon, though I don't know why I was suddenly put into solitary. Very minimal food was provided in all Gestapo jails, and the food we did receive was all vile. I was handed a hunk of dry bread in the morning and watery soup three times a day. Their bread was baked with sawdust to give it weight, and the soup was a thin broth with a few vegetables floating in it.

I was starving all the time, but I would still treasure my hunk of bread for many hours before finally eating it slowly at night. This was the only way I could sleep through the night without being kept awake by hunger.

I lost a near-fatal amount of weight at this time. I was weighed in Besançon: I was 92 pounds. Before that, I had weighed about 135 pounds. For my height of five feet eight inches, I had become extremely thin.

From Besançon, I was transferred to the city of Dijon, about one hundred kilometres away. As I walked into the jail, an SS man rushed at me, screaming, "Sind Sie Jude? Sind Sie Jude?" (Are you a Jew? Are you a Jew?) I looked him in the eye and said, "Nein." (No.) I answered him so coolly that he didn't question or examine me further.

The Dijon jail must have been the worst jail in France. It was a gloomy, medieval place. Even though they thought we were Belgian and so we weren't treated like Jews, which would have been even worse, the guards beat us constantly. After I had spent a week in that jail, a transport was assembled to send us to Belgium. We were put on an ordinary train in special cars guarded by German soldiers and German police. There was one guard for every two prisoners. Prisoners weren't handcuffed, but a German guard went with us wherever we went, even to the toilet. It was a slow train, which made for a long trip.

I thought continually about escaping and tried to develop a plan. I thought about making a run for it, but I didn't take the step. A number of times I thought of leaping from a toilet window or opening a compartment door and jumping out. The Germans were watching so closely that there wasn't much chance of succeeding.

We arrived in Lille in the evening and had to change trains for Brussels. We were herded off the train, then led from one platform to another when, suddenly, a guy who I suspected was Jewish disappeared. I saw him go, but the station was so crowded with people that he vanished into the throng. The Germans couldn't follow and lost him.

I told myself, *That guy did the right thing. I should do that, too.* I tried to figure out how to do it, when to do it, but opportunities were limited. When we boarded the train for Brussels, I kept thinking, *Should I jump?* If I went through to Brussels with a false identity card, I was a doomed man. I knew the only chance I had was to escape.

For one reason or another, I didn't jump, I didn't run. There were few chances to attempt an escape, but even knowing that sometimes we have to make our own chances, I didn't do anything.

We pulled into Brussels and were lugged away to Saint-Gilles prison. It was the worst prison I had been in yet. There were about three thousand political prisoners incarcerated there, and I could hear continuous barking and screaming. I was locked in a cell and kept there for about a week. I was then summoned for interrogation with some other prisoners. We were led to a large room partitioned into separate cubicles. In each one, an SS man presided at a table.

I realized I had to make a good impression, to give the appearance that I was telling the truth. A booth became empty; my turn was next. The interrogator in that booth was an older man who looked experienced. I was sure he would quickly see through me, so I held back to try to avoid him.

In a moment, another booth was free. The interrogator there was a youth of eighteen or nineteen, and I thrust myself toward him. I told him my story. I had to play a strange game: I purported to be a Belgian, but my name wasn't Walloon, French Belgian; it was Flemish, and I couldn't speak Flemish, which is Belgian Dutch and somewhat different from the Dutch language spoken in the Netherlands. So I always spoke to the Germans in broken German to forestall their calling an interpreter who would have realized immediately that I wasn't who I said I was.

I talked to this young SS man in broken German. I told him about my brother and the milk business in Lyon. Then I watched as he wrote, "Der Angeklagte macht einen glaubwürdigen Eindruck." (The accused gives the impression that he is telling the truth.) After that, I was hurried back to my cell.

Again I sat in a jail with filthy conditions. Saint-Gilles was full of lice like the French jails. I thought, *I'll never get out of this hole.* They would wake us at five o'clock in the morning, and then we did absolutely nothing for the rest of the day. We were given almost nothing to eat — I was dangerously thin and it surprised me that I didn't catch tuberculosis or some other wasting disease.

I had almost given up hope. Prisoners were being shot every night in the courtyard. I could hear the shots and the screams.

If the Gestapo discovered that someone was a Jew, they shot the person immediately. I thought, *They'll come at any moment — they'll discover I'm a Jew because my identity card is false. How can Wavre confirm that I'm Jan Van Capelle and that I used to live there? The address probably doesn't even exist. And the name with my personal statistics certainly doesn't exist.*

One day, about two weeks after I arrived there, the *Feldwebel*, a sergeant, appeared and shouted, "Van Capelle!" I said to myself, *This is it, the day of reckoning.*

I sat, hesitating. The sergeant snapped, "Come out! Fast!" Everything had to be done in quick time.

He ordered, "Take your stuff!"

I said to myself, *Oh, no. It's over.*

He shrilled, "Why don't you come faster? You're free!"

I couldn't believe it. Free! How could I be free? Free!

I didn't believe him. Impossible. But I couldn't reveal what I thought.

Then the process of freeing me started. It took six hours until I'd gone round to all the different offices and officials to get checked and signed out and released through all those doors, doors, doors.

And there I was one evening at the end of December 1942, a free man in Brussels. A German Jew. Via the Netherlands. Via Switzerland. Via France. I was free in Brussels! I didn't know anyone. I had never lived in Belgium. A war was on. What was I supposed to do now?

Moving Underground

When the Germans set me free from Saint-Gilles, they gave me a warning and a letter of instruction: I was to report to the police chief in Wavre within twenty-four hours. If I failed to report in Wavre, I would be arrested again.

But I couldn't report to Wavre. It was just a dot on the map to me. I had never been there. I knew that, even without civil records and official inquiries, the police chief would easily discover that my identity was false. I decided I'd better get out of Brussels or disappear underground.

Another prisoner who had been released from Saint-Gilles at the same time was going to the Gare du Nord, a train station in Brussels, to take a train home. I tagged along with him and noticed a Salvation Army hostel near the Gare du Nord. When we reached the station, I said goodbye to the other fellow.

It had grown dark by this time. Retracing my steps, I went to the Salvation Army hostel and was welcomed in. They gave me a bowl of soup and told me I could sleep there for one night.

The following day, I walked around Brussels wondering what to do next. All kinds of schemes entered my head. I thought of finding some Jews. I saw a man on the street who I thought was a Jew and followed him. He tried to avoid me, but I collared him. Shoving him into a corner, I grabbed him by the throat and said, "I know that you're a Jew; don't deny it. I'm a Jew, too. I want you to help me. You have to give me shelter or tell me where to find other Jews. I'm here alone. I don't know anybody."

He was scared and he tried to shake me off. Finally, he gave me an address and told me how to get there.

I arrived at the address and discovered the offices of the Association of Jews in Belgium, which was similar to a Jewish Council. I went in. The people there told me the situation in Brussels was desperate for Jews and the only thing to do was give myself up. This was the same advice I had received from the Jewish Council in the Netherlands — surrender to the Germans! I realized I was in a trap and escaped from the spot as fast as I could. Luckily, I got away, even though the Germans could have been watching the place.

I decided then that I would never again have anything to do with the Jewish Councils or similar organizations. I would never go near them again. I would never appeal to them for help. I wanted nothing to do with them. I wanted nothing from them.

Then I remembered the Austrian couple I had met through Piefke's uncle and whose flat Piefke and I had visited. So, racking my memory, I traced my way to the statue of Manneken Pis and from there I managed to find the flat.

The woman remembered me; she was very friendly and kind. Her husband had been arrested by the Gestapo, but she was in a fairly safe position because she had a German passport, since Hitler had annexed Austria in 1938. As a German and a gentile, she wasn't under suspicion.

However, this woman was actually active in the Belgian underground. That night she took me to stay at another flat. Then she spread the word about me to others in the resistance. I was shuffled from one flat to another for several nights.

A few days later, I decided to venture outside Brussels to the suburb where Piefke's uncle lived. I wanted to try to locate him and maybe Piefke.

His uncle wasn't there anymore, and the neighbours had no news of him or Piefke, but they recognized me and were pleased to see me. They invited me into their house. I had left my phylacteries with them, and right away the woman went to a cupboard and returned soon saying, "Here. Here are your holy objects." She didn't know what to call them. "Here they are," she said. "Do you want to take them with you?"

I said, "No, thanks very much. I can't take them with me. I don't know where I'm going." After a short visit, I headed back to the city.

The people I was staying with in Brussels were all in the Belgian resistance movement called the Witte Brigade. At first, they were suspicious of me, thinking I might be a spy. I told them that I wasn't really Jan Van Capelle, though I used that name. I said my real name was Eli Hart and that I was Dutch.

The Austrian woman accepted me for what I said I was since she'd met me under that name when I had first come from the Netherlands. Then, quizzing me themselves, the others became very interested in me after I told them about my Swiss and other jail experiences. They wanted people like me to join the underground army to do illegal work and sabotage.

They induced me to join them. "After a while," they emphasized, "all of us will go to England to be trained as commandos for the eventual invasion of Europe." This prospect appealed to me — I was longing to become a fighter of some sort. Connected with them, I could look forward to serving in the regular British Army, the commandos or some other force, and fighting the Nazis in the open.

Therefore, I attached myself to the Witte Brigade, which also seemed to be the only way to sustain myself. There were few means of surviving unless one was part of an organization.

Our group always met on the Rue Verte near the Gare du Nord, a slummy red-light district with a floating sea of unsavoury types and questionable enterprises. It was the least conspicuous place for the underground to meet.

Our group organized and carried out raids and attacks, particularly to obtain ration tickets. Everybody had to have ration tickets simply to buy basic food, and most underground people didn't have them. We stole the stamps from the administrative offices that issued them. In the daytime, when the offices were open, we would rush in waving pistols and demand all the tickets, moving quickly and getting away fast.

We were armed with pistols for show, but we didn't use force unless we had to. The people we confronted usually knew they couldn't resist us successfully, so they handed over the tickets without commotion. Some officials actually cooperated with us; they were probably sympathetic to our cause. Others tried to resist. Sometimes there were German guards on duty at the locations. We tried to avoid them by either striking when they weren't around or sneaking in and out through a back or side door so they wouldn't detect us.

We also set explosives at bridges, tunnels and railway overpasses. Our goal was to disrupt the transportation system to stop the German movement of ammunition and soldiers.

I teamed up with people who were experts in explosives, some of whom were engineers. Most often I acted as a lookout for them, and they did the skilled work that I wasn't trained to do. My job was to guard them, alert them and cover their retreat.

These manoeuvres were offensive attacks. We tried to do the utmost damage to the Germans and were ready to shoot if we were in danger. At times we had to use our pistols, but this made us especially vulnerable because the Germans were equipped with superior weapons. Shooting was our last resort.

Sometimes we ambushed and shot at German staff cars to try to kill specific officers. It was difficult to know how many we hit because we had to escape from the scene quickly. I was always ready, however, to fire another shot to make sure we completed our mission. These activities all took place in Brussels or close to it.

After a while, we reduced the amount of railway sabotage we did

because the Germans retaliated by executing disproportionate numbers of local people. This was too high a price to pay.

After a couple of months our group of fifteen had become a hot
target. In late February 1943, the leaders decided to ship us to England.

We gathered one evening in the basement of a house on the Rue
Verte. We were celebrating our imminent departure, as that night we
were going to drive to a place near Antwerp where a plane would
land, pick us up and transport us to England.

I'd spent all my Belgian money that afternoon. There wasn't much
one could buy in those days, so I bought some silly things just to get
rid of the currency, since I thought I'd be in England the next day.

I'd developed the habit of studying every building I entered to
devise ways of quickly leaving it. I'd learned that it was often easy
to enter an establishment, but difficult to get out, especially to get
out fast. The house we were assembled in that night was one I'd been
scrutinizing for some time.

We were enjoying the party, happy and optimistic about our travel plans. We ate and drank wine, toasting the group. Our leader, a
French officer, was with us. Among us were Soviets and other Eastern
Europeans who had escaped from prisoner-of-war camps or deserted
the Axis troops. We were all shipping out together.

Suddenly, we heard German boots stamping down the steps.
Stamp! Stamp! Stamp! We heard them break through the basement
door, and we heard shots being fired.

The moment I heard boots, I jumped straight up. I knew that
sound, its meaning: get out or be shot. We would all be dead.

I rushed up the inside stairs of the house just as the Germans
burst into the basement. The place rattled with gunfire. The Germans
had machine guns and heavy ammunition, and we had only small
pistols to fight them off.

The building we were in was three or four storeys high. I raced
to the top floor as fast as I could. I knew there was a ledge outside
a window — it was the top of a small wall jutting into a courtyard. I

thought I would just sit near the window, and if they came after me, I'd get out and hide on the ledge. All this took only a few minutes. I heard continuous shooting. Then the boots started up the stairs, stomping into every room.

I clambered out on the ledge. Figures appeared at the window and shone strong lights everywhere. They spotted me and yelled, "Gib auf!" (Surrender!)

The moment I heard that, I jumped down from the high ledge to the courtyard below. I didn't know where I would land.

In European cities, the interior courtyards surrounded by buildings and walls are paved with brick or stone. I could have broken my back or legs on the pavement or seriously injured myself — in the moment, I didn't feel anything. I had little time to think. A German came out on the ledge right after I had jumped, shone his flashlight on me and started to shoot.

There were several doors leading into the courtyard. I thought, *I'll run for a door and try it. If it opens, I'll be able to get away — if it's locked, I'm trapped, cornered.*

The German kept shooting at me as I scurried toward a door and pushed hard. It opened! I fled through the door into a house. I was in a dark hallway. I ran to the other end of it toward another door. I knew that I had to get out of there. They would likely surround the area, and it might have been surrounded already.

I opened the front door and stepped onto a street opposite the Rue Verte. I kept on going, going, going. Then I saw a streetcar and jumped on. After a few stops, I transferred to another streetcar going in a different direction. I did this several times until I was far from the Rue Verte.

I thought maybe I had been hit somewhere. I was wearing a beret; I removed it. There were five bullet holes in it, but I wasn't hit. This was the closest call that I'd had for some time.

People were often being betrayed. Someone must have spilled our plans or unwittingly betrayed us. The French captain who led us was frequently involved with prostitutes on the Rue Verte. Some prostitutes acted as informers for the Germans, and I suspected that one of them had betrayed us to the Gestapo.

~

My career in the underground resistance was over. I couldn't operate effectively in that sphere anymore. I was now bent on returning to farming, which is what I'd intended to do immediately after my release from Saint-Gilles.

I went to see the Austrian woman again and I told her what had happened. She agreed with my decision. She made inquiries and put me in contact with a Dutchman named Dirk.

Dirk was a painter who'd married a Belgian woman and settled in Belgium. He had the ruddy face and blond hair of Dutchmen depicted in many Flemish and Dutch paintings. He was a burly, jolly, happy-go-lucky man. When I met him, he offered to help me find a job on a farm. He was living north of Brussels beyond Laeken in an outer suburb called Strombeek-Bever. One Sunday morning, we canvassed the neighbourhood farms together. Dirk persuaded a farmer and his wife to hire me, and so I went to work for them.

I found a room to rent with a very poor family near the farm; my room cost a trifle, yet it was income for these people. Being able to eat on the farm was a major advantage of farm work, since I still didn't have ration tickets.

The farming was mixed: there were animals and extensive crop land. The farmer was getting rich by selling on the black market. Grain brought high prices, so workers were denied an extra slice of bread. The farmer's wife was especially miserly and a brutal boss: she wanted maximum work for a minimum amount of food. In her view, the farmhands never worked hard enough and always ate too much. It was a wretched place.

I often visited Dirk. He was always in a cheerful mood and would laugh and ridicule all the privations on the farm. He was extremely generous, always offering me a meal. Since I didn't have ration tickets, he shared his rations with me.

Sanitary conditions on the farm were also deplorable. One day my left hand began to swell larger and larger. I bathed it in hot water and swallowed pills given to me by a farmhand, but there was no improvement. After a while, I realized that I had to see a doctor. My hand had become huge and distorted. I appealed to Dirk, whose sister-in-law recommended a young doctor in a district close to where I worked.

I went to the doctor, and he told me he had to cut it open right away, otherwise I might lose my hand. I had blood poisoning. He made an incision on the back of my left hand between the last two fingers. A gush of blood mixed with pus and dirt spurted out. With no antibiotics available, the hand needed slow, painstaking cleansing. It took more than three days of repeated washing for the infected matter to drain away completely.

After approximately a week, my hand healed. The doctor had operated superbly, and I was deeply grateful for what he had done. If Dirk and his sister-in-law hadn't directed me to the doctor, I might have lost my hand. What would I have done then? I doubt that I could have survived the war with only one hand.

Manure must have invaded a pimple or blister and infected it. Working in the poorly maintained stable, I had no way to keep my hands clean.

The last two fingers of my left hand did not fully regain their strength. For a while, I thought I had lost the ability to milk: milking requires two strong hands, as pressure has to be applied equally with both. My weak left hand slowed my work for some time, but slowly I retrained it, and the hand recovered its strength.

By the time my hand had completely healed and had regained its strength, I realized that I was fed up with this farmer and his stingy wife. They knew I was Jewish and acted nervous and scared and let me know every day that I wasn't welcome there. The man was working again in the coal mines nearby, and so my rent was no longer essential for them.

I decided to take a chance somewhere else. I heard talk of a shortage of farm labourers on the other side of Brussels at Waterloo, so I headed there by streetcar. At that time, Waterloo was a quiet, rural town set in rich, rolling farmland. I walked down the main street, Chaussée de Bruxelles, and stopped at a farm called la ferme de Mont-Saint-Jean. I asked for work, but no help was needed there.

I walked on past the *gendarmerie*, police station, and stopped at another farm. I asked the farmer if he needed any help. He asked, "You know how to milk?" He led me into the barn and told me, "Sit down and milk."

I sat down, and he gave me a pail. He watched as I milked and saw that I milked very well. "Good," he said. "You've got a job."

Jobs were easy to find at that time in Waterloo because the Germans had picked up many young Belgian men and sent them to work in Germany, creating a serious shortage of farmhands. Even so, the farmer in Waterloo was unable to provide me with a bedroom. Since I wanted to live on the farm, at least for a while, I suggested to the farmer that I could sleep in the stable, and he agreed.

And so I slept in the stable, making up my bed of straw in the corner each night. Sometimes the animals got loose and could have trampled me. Although the situation was precarious in that respect, I felt comfortable there.

The farmhouse, kitchen, garden and barns were in the centre of Waterloo. The fields were on the edge of town. Fernand, the farmer, was a young fellow whose father had recently died. He and his elderly mother were running the farm together and needed a great deal of help.

They kept thirty or forty milking cows. I did all the milking by myself. Sometimes they joined me to clean the stables, but they couldn't do this when they had work to do in the fields.

Because I did nothing else, I was able to handle the work by myself. I was happy to work all the time. Unfortunately, I couldn't visit Dirk. I couldn't saunter in the streets because of the frequent heavily armed German patrols in the district.

My one diversion was going to the movies: I went on Sundays before the afternoon milking. The town cinema was on the main street close to the farm. I saw many French films starring the actresses Danielle Darrieux, Edwige Feuillère and Michèle Morgan, among others.

People were resisting openly in the Waterloo area, with several uprisings occurring at this time and even frequent shootings in the streets. When I drove the cows out to pasture and brought them back in for milking, I would pass by a house behind the communal administration building that I recognized as being used by the resistance. With rebellion so close to the surface, the Germans were massing troops in the area to subdue the population. It was a very volatile spot.

In Waterloo, the lice in my hair were again a plague. My hair grew fast in those days, and I had to have it cut often. I would sit in the barber's chair thinking, *What if he sees the lice? He'll notice the nits — I'm covered in them! He'll throw me out.* The barber wouldn't tolerate lice on his combs and scissors, as they could infest a barbershop.

I finally decided to do something about the lice. I went to a pharmacy in Waterloo and asked for a remedy. The pharmacist gave me some powder, and I used it again and again all over my body. After a while, their numbers seemed to lower and then gradually the lice disappeared. It took a long time to control them because I was still sleeping in the unsanitary stable. I also wasn't changing my clothes enough — I simply couldn't, I didn't have many clothes. Yet I managed to overcome the lice.

I had another stubborn problem at the time. After I moved to Waterloo, a boil developed on my neck. Then I was plagued with boils — large, ugly, painful swellings. They ballooned on my neck and the back of my head. I had one boil after another, a constant affliction, and I had no treatment for them. I let them ripen until they burst, then squeezed them. Pus poured from them like water.

Even now, so many decades later, there are marks on my neck and head where the boils had been. People suggested they were associated with my age, since young adults are susceptible to skin eruptions. But the boils were unusually severe, so I'm inclined to think they were related to either poor hygiene or malnutrition.

I walked through Waterloo with the cattle every day, driving them from the stable to the pasture and then from the pasture back to the stable. The Germans had set up posts to check everybody but they never questioned me. I went through their check posts time and time again, and they didn't ask me anything. I was Jan Van Capelle, *vacher*, cowherd. I was so shabbily dressed and insignificant looking that the Germans never stopped me.

I didn't tell anyone in Waterloo that I was a Jew. In Strombeek-Bever, the people I'd worked for and those I had lived with knew I was Jewish. After my experience with them, I stopped identifying myself as a Jew because I'd observed that people were uneasy, tense and irritable, just having me around. It seemed to make them feel guilty. Or maybe they were fearful that they themselves would be arrested.

I decided that I wasn't going to mention it again. It was the best way to proceed. It was April 1943, and from then on, I lost my identity completely.

I worked extremely hard in Waterloo with never enough to eat. Three slices of bread was the most I was allowed at a meal, and I could have eaten six. I compensated for this by milking directly into my own mouth. Drinking milk straight from the udder never made me sick, possibly because I had developed immunity to the bacteria. The boils, however, may have resulted from drinking the milk this way. But it was necessary to keep my strength up, and I soon grew accustomed to working so hard.

Even though I found out later the situation had been quite different, from what I was hearing at the time, the Germans had by now conquered most of the Soviet Union and were successful even in Africa. I couldn't conceive of the war ending with anything other than a German victory. It seemed to me sometimes that my struggle was all in vain, that I was straining myself to the limit and that I couldn't win. I wasn't optimistic.

What drove me on, however, was the thought of my own premature death. I decided to do whatever I could to hang on to life, to simply stay alive as long as I could. I would continue to scramble through, to see if I could escape whatever decrees the Nazis would make for Jews. I didn't really believe I would succeed, but one thing was certain: I was never going to surrender. I was never going to give myself up to be delivered to a concentration camp. This resolve was foremost in my mind. All my effort was aimed at avoiding the concentration camps. And if I ever did get taken to a concentration camp, I was determined to carry at least one dead German on my back.

Fernand, the young farmer in Waterloo, was hoping to get married and took up with several girls. He began to count on having me around. I relieved him of many tasks, and he let me take charge of my own work on the farm.

Then he married. His wife moved into the house and proved to be much nicer than him or his mother. She saw that I had few clothes, so she gave me Fernand's old pants and shirts. She was very considerate and tried to help me as much as she could.

I had nowhere safe to put my money, so always kept it with me, hidden in a pocket of my jacket or under my pillow at night. I had also carried my mother's bracelet on me for several years. I kept it through all the jails without its being discovered. In one jail, the Gestapo took my jacket away, but when they returned it to me, the bracelet was still in the pocket.

One day in Waterloo, the woman asked me to dig up her vegetable garden. I dug it up and somehow lost the bracelet. Though I looked for it carefully, I couldn't find it. I never found it after that.

In the early fall of 1943, there was a bumper crop of sugar beets, which had to be dug out of the ground by hand. Crews of contract workers travelled from farm to farm throughout Belgium to bring in the harvest. A crew came to the farm where I was and worked in the fields for long hours. I would talk with them at night.

I became friendly with the leader of the crew, who asked me in surprise, "Why do you stay in this hole? What are you doing here? It's a miserable job and you never get enough to eat." I had told him about the three slices of bread I received, and he saw it with his own eyes. He said, "They're rotten people. All they want is to make loads of money on the black market." The farm's location gave them easy access to the black-market trade in Brussels.

"You get nothing out of this job," he said to me. "Why don't you go to Liège in the eastern part of Belgium? You'll find big farms there and nice people and get a good job. The way you work, you'll get the best job in Belgium! You have nothing to worry about."

I didn't make a move for a while. I had no legal papers and knew it would be dangerous for me to move across Belgium. The farmers there might not hire someone without papers. Since my release from Saint-Gilles, the identity card had become useless, as my Belgian alias was probably on a Gestapo list.

But in October of 1943, I had reached the limit with three slices of bread, unending work and sleeping in the stable. It simply wasn't right. Living like that was so demeaning that I thought, *I'm barely surviving. Who knows how much longer this war will last?* I couldn't see an end in sight.

There were employment agencies at the time that placed workers with farmers needing hands. The migrant workers gave me the name of an agent in the region near Liège.

I wrote to the agent. He answered and told me to go to a specific farm. I decided that I would take the chance. Maybe I would find a different way of life. So in hopes of improving my situation, after six months of sleeping in that stable I was on the move again.

Unlikely Saviour

I carried a bag with a few clothes in it over my shoulder like a potato sack and left Waterloo.

From Brussels, I took a train via Leuven. West of Liège, I disembarked at the small station of Fexhe-le-Haut-Clocher and asked the station master for directions to the farm. His reply indicated that I was expected there. I walked a zigzag route from the station through a pretty town of low red and brown brick buildings. The fields belonging to the farm stretched beyond an old church.

The brick farm buildings were constructed like a fortress. The barns, stables, sheds and handsome farmhouse formed a quadrangle around an inner courtyard. In the middle of the courtyard lay a large manure pile, which strangely enough exuded no smell. Surrounding the buildings, gardens and fields extended to the far distance.

The farm was stocked with horses, cows and bulls — about forty horses and forty or fifty cows and calves. The farmer was breeding steers and horses and had many young animals. It was very progressive farming.

I was hired by the farmer and immediately given a room in the attic of the farmhouse. It was small with little in it, but at least it was a room. It was decent, civilized.

I began my work as a milker. Whenever I saw the farmer, Monsieur Roberti, in the first week I was there, I thought that he looked unwell. He was a young man, about thirty-five years of age, with a wife and two children.

The farmer died suddenly at the end of the week. The whole place became unsettled. Farmhands gossiped about whether or not the widow could manage the farm by herself.

I focused on milking. With Monsieur Roberti gone, I was left alone. The widow, Madeleine, helped me irregularly.

A short time later, her father and mother, Monsieur and Madame Degive, arrived from Liège. Retired and over sixty years old, Monsieur Degive was a stern-looking man. He had injured a leg and now limped, but he had been a prosperous farmer, a breeder of horses and bulls. Now, faced with his daughter's predicament, he came out of retirement to take charge of the farm.

After a while it became too much for the widow to help with the milking; she had many other things to do. Instead, she gave me more responsibility and asked the maid Claire to help me. Claire was the daughter of Polish immigrants. Her father worked in the mines near Liège. She had grown up in Belgium and spoke fluent French. She had blond hair and a pale, round face with broad high cheekbones.

Claire wasn't trained, so I taught her how to milk, and she soon acquired the skill. She helped me every day and especially on Sunday, because on that day we stopped work early. On weekends when Claire went to visit her parents, the widow helped with Sunday's milking.

I was a very skilled milker. I had learned from the Friesians, the best milkers in the world, and these Belgian farmers took notice of it and respected me for my work. I milked and cleaned the stables. I worked all the time and never went out. If the farmers were suspicious of my cloistered life, they never talked to me about it.

Monsieur Degive became interested in me. I was the only worker who stayed overnight. Many were married and lived in the village. At night, the farm was a medieval stronghold. The animals were in the stables and a solid wooden gate closed the farm off completely. One day the old man gave me the farm key and told me to open the gate every morning and close it every night, so I became the gatekeeper.

The first thing I observed on this farm was that I could eat as much as I wanted. Although the farms in Waterloo were productive, that part of Belgium around Liège was a rich area, and people were much more generous. If they were concerned about the black market, it wasn't obvious to me. Maybe its importance to them was on a large scale, not just to sell a few extra slices of bread or glasses of milk.

Madame Degive sincerely grew to like me. She taught me how to bake bread. Once a week, every Friday, she baked thirty-two enormous round loaves in an outdoor oven. I was the one who always helped her place the bread on long handles straight into the oven and then pulled the handles out.

In the evenings, I ate with the other farmhands in a room off the kitchen. After they'd eaten and left, the old woman would call me into the kitchen and give me another meal — a better one than the workers ate that came from part of the family's meal. She would tell me to polish her grandsons' shoes, which allowed me to work for the extra food she gave me. But having me clean the shoes was just a pretext.

Later in the evenings the boys would come visit me. They were lively youngsters, about eight and ten years of age. I would tell them stories, and they were so keen! Every night while I polished their shoes, they ran to me to hear another story.

I told them stories by the Grimm brothers, from Wilhelm Busch's *Max and Moritz* and from the Bible. I also made up stories, even though I was sometimes hard pressed to think up a new one. I noticed that after a while even the old man was listening to my stories.

Sometimes I helped the boys with their schoolwork, and in doing this probably I revealed too much of myself. I certainly showed that I was more intelligent than I appeared to be and that I wasn't the person I pretended to be. The old man may have talked to his wife about it — he knew there was more to me than first appeared. But no one ever said a word to me about it.

∼

When I opened the gate in the morning, the old farmer sometimes came out and talked to me. One morning he said, "You know, Jan, I'd like to have your papers. I can clear you so you don't get sent to work in Germany. You can stay here. I have good contacts and will be able to fix it up completely. Don't worry, I can clear you."

I answered, "Ah…" I began to tell him a tale. "I don't have my papers," I said. "I left them with my uncle in Brussels."

Twice he asked me for my papers, then he gave up. He realized that I had no usable papers and he never mentioned it again, nor did he ever ask me anything more about who I was. Monsieur Degive knew that there was something clandestine about me. But he took a chance on me.

I established a close relationship with him. He was a very intelligent man and saw some potential in me. He went out of his way to be kind to me and tried to teach me skills that he knew well. For instance, he asked me if I would like to learn something about horses, since he was an experienced horse breeder.

Sometimes we sat up together all night waiting for a mare to foal. A horse's birth is very difficult, especially if the foal comes out legs first. The old man taught me how to pull out the foal, when to pull and when not to pull. I appreciated his excellent instructions, and he could tell I was interested in learning. He also taught me how to breed bulls. He was a renowned bull breeder, and explained to me in detail the qualities and features to look for in a bull.

He owned a magnificent bull. Other farmers came to have their cows inseminated by the bull, and he put me in charge of this service, of handling the bull myself, and didn't trust any of the others to do this. Whenever a cow was to be impregnated, I had to run with the bull, lift up the cow's tail and control the bull.

Other farmhands were afraid of the bull, but the old man told me, "Once the bull knows you, you don't have to worry about him. Don't be frightened of him. He won't do anything to you." And the old man was right; he knew.

With thirty or forty milking cows and many young cattle to care for, I performed a demanding job. Still, the attitude and trust of Monsieur Degive more than compensated me. He did a lot more for me than he had to.

I was much happier there than I'd been on other farms. I was well fed and housed and made to feel like a human being. I worked very hard, although not harder than in Waterloo, and the treatment I received was better. I could even put my earnings under my mattress and leave them untouched for weeks.

These farmers were members of the nearby Catholic church; everyone in the area was Catholic. The priest would visit the farm on his rounds and ask me why I wasn't attending church. The only explanation I could think of was, "I have so much to do; I don't feel like going to church." He asked me once or twice but didn't insist.

Some of the other workers, too, asked why I never went to church. Subtle pressures were put on me to become more involved with them socially or to go out with girls.

I did often banter with Claire. She was cheerful and bright; she caught on to things fast. However, I didn't want to get involved with any girls — the situation was too unstable — so no intimacy ever developed between us.

Claire never invited me to her parents' home. I never even went to Liège, which was only ten kilometres away, although some of the farmhands invited me to come with them for a beer or go out with them on the weekends. I always shrugged off these invitations. I didn't want to expose myself to police checks or raids.

After a while, the old couple decided I was working too hard and should have some help. Someone was picked to help me clean out the stables each day. We became good friends. He was a bachelor who lived in a village nearby and owned a small farm of his own. He was independent, but worked for the widow to protect himself from deportation to Germany. He obtained grain and feed for his animals through this work and earned extra money.

This fellow always reported to me what he'd heard on Radio London. He listened in the evening when Radio London was broadcasting in French to Belgium and told me the latest news each morning. I followed the course of the war through him and wouldn't have known what was happening otherwise, and he also kept me informed on activities and events in the region.

I'd been wearing the farmer's old shirts, and none of them fit me properly. I finally thought about buying a new shirt for myself. My friend said he could buy me a shirt on the black market, so I told him to go ahead. He bought a rough shirt of heavy, coarse material with wide green and brown stripes on a white background. I paid four hundred francs for it — a month's wages. I'd worked fourteen to sixteen hours a day for thirty days to earn enough to buy the shirt. Yet, in normal times, I wouldn't have worn such a shirt and would be ashamed to wear it today.

This bachelor would occasionally invite me to his home, to play cards or just visit, but nothing ever came of it. There were several villages to pass through on the way to his home, and I would have had to come back late at night on my own. Without papers, I didn't want to risk it.

One day the fellow said, "You know, our farmer here is very close to the Germans." This was a revelation to me, but people in the district were talking about it.

Some time later, I was sitting by myself in the stable milking the cows when trucks swung into the courtyard. I heard motors spinning, clatter, and German voices. I tried to crouch between the cows, hoping I wouldn't be seen. But the Germans saw me.

"Get up! Get up! Get up!" was the command. "Where are your papers? Who are you? What are you doing here?"

They were grabbing at me and scouring the place. It was a *razzia*.

I said, "Wait… look… my papers are upstairs in my room." The officer signalled to a soldier to go with me to check my papers.

The soldier and I went up to my room and I looked around there as if I were searching for papers. Then the German said something I'll never forget.

"Du bist doch ein armer Teufel." (You're such a poor devil). "Why don't you go to Germany? Your room is so bare. You have nothing here. You're so poor you don't even have a pair of good pants. You have nothing. In Germany you would be much better off."

I answered, "Sure… but I was born here. I came from here."

He rejoined, "You know, it's…" He spoke to me half in German, half in French. When I showed that I understood German, he forgot about my papers!

Suddenly the sergeant-major walked in announcing, "Okay, everything's okay. Let's go. I checked all the papers downstairs. Everything's in order."

What papers had the farmer shown him? I don't know what happened and never found out. The old man never mentioned it to me, and I never talked to him about it. A strange relationship existed between him and me.

The old man owned a special horse and carriage that he used for visitors. One day he remarked to me, "Jan, you're now in charge of the carriage. You're going to drive it whenever I need you." Sometimes he had guests in the evening after the other workers had gone home.

The first time I drove the carriage he told me to drive to the station to pick up a German general. He said, "The general knows I'm sending you for him — I told him Jan will pick him up."

So there I was with a comely little horse and carriage. I drove to the station, tied up the horse and stood at the exit. The general arrived with his adjutant. They saw me and greeted me, "Jan! Jan!"

The general was in high spirits. He and the adjutant shook my hand. They both climbed into the carriage and I drove them to the farm. I let them out of the carriage, and the general gave me ten francs as a tip before he and his assistant entered the house.

I heard laughter and toasts over wine from the dining room that night. There was feasting and drinking and merriment. They stayed overnight. At six o'clock the next morning, I was again ready with the horse and carriage. The general gave me another tip after I took them back to the station.

I repeated these trips many times, for many weeks in a row. The general arrived by train every Wednesday night. I drove him from and to the station. He came for dinner and stayed overnight. He was the military commander of Liège. Obviously, my friend the bachelor had spoken the truth: the shrewd old farmer had powerful German connections.

By now we were well into 1944. On June 6, the American and British and other Allied forces landed in Normandy, France. Workers on the farm couldn't stop talking about it.

From then on, my bachelor friend had exciting reports for me daily. He informed me when the Germans were retreating and when the underground had begun to be more active. He conveyed the smallest details to me. He pinpointed the Allied advance. "The Americans and the British are coming here. They'll soon be here."

As the Allied armies approached Belgium, more local resistance to the Germans began to emerge. One night, members of the resistance occupied our farm and captured German soldiers found wandering in the fields — deserters from the German army, mainly Poles or Baltic nationals who'd volunteered or were pressed into military service. My impulse was to join the resistance at the first opportunity. I wanted to be involved in the action. But the resistance fighters left swiftly in the middle of the night.

The Germans swept back. They burned down farm after farm trying to smoke out members of the resistance, who kept moving around the countryside. The farm next to ours was flattened completely; the Roberti farm wasn't touched, presumably because our boss had the right contacts.

Slowly, the tenor was changing. The course of the war was changing. One day my co-worker told me the Americans were near, already lodging in the area and turning up everywhere in Jeeps.

Then one day an American Jeep drove into our courtyard. Four Americans were in it. They asked for directions. I was standing in the courtyard with the widow. When I saw the Americans enter, I couldn't conceal my joy. The war was coming to an end! An end to a tangle of problems.

I talked to the Americans in English. I lost my self-control and forgot myself completely. I hadn't spoken English for about six years. I'd never spoken to an American, but even with their accents I had no difficulty understanding them.

The Americans were surprised when I spoke English. The widow was speechless. I showed the Americans around the farm and told them a little about it. A short while later they left. I remained on the farm doing my job as usual.

The Germans slowly pulled out and left the area. The Americans moved in but were still advancing, so resistance groups took over and administered everything. The resistance began to mete out punishment and arrest all types of collaborators. Women who had fraternized with German soldiers were publicly humiliated. One day, thirty or forty resistance fighters carrying guns drove into the farm and pulled up in front of the house. They wanted to arrest the old farmer!

Monsieur Degive was standing mute on the front steps.

Suddenly he pointed at me and said, "Ask that man what I've done for him, which side I've really been on, whose side I've been on all along."

The resistance commander turned to me. He walked over and questioned me. "Yeah," I affirmed. "I've been hiding here for almost a year. He protected me. It's only because of him that I'm still alive. What he says is true."

There must have been some speculation and gossip about me locally because the commander and his men believed what I said; they believed the old man and me. The leader ordered his men to withdraw and they left without further question.

The old man never once mentioned the incident to me afterwards.

I kept on helping Madame Degive with the bread. She continued to give me a double supper. Everything went on as usual.

A few weeks later, damaged railway lines were repaired, and train travel to Brussels was re-established. I advised Monsieur Degive that I was anxious to visit my uncle in Brussels. The old man knew immediately that I would never come back. His wife knew it, too. They said to me, "Sure. Of course. Goodbye. Bye. Bye."

I saw in their faces that they knew I would never come back. They knew, too, that I wasn't Jan Van Capelle. They had known for some time that I wasn't the person I pretended to be. But they never asked who I was, never asked me where I'd come from, and I really appreciated that.

The old farmer had saved my life, and I'd saved his. Our time together was finished, it would seem, but I owed him much more than he owed me. He was old; I was young, just twenty-two, with my adult life ahead of me.

Admittedly, I'd worked non-stop, every day of the week. As I mentioned, I never went out. Workers used to comment, "You work so hard. Why don't you go out on weekends? Have a little fun." Most of them didn't understand what my situation was, but Monsieur Degive understood. And within these narrow limits, he made my life very tolerable. I owe him a great debt for this.

His wife, too, was unusually kind, even though she was a tough woman. Both of them were tough and stern, but on the scale of virtues, they rated very high.

They liked me so much that they wanted me to stay there permanently. To encourage this, they tried to stimulate a relationship between the maid and me: if I would marry Claire, the old woman suggested, they would set us up in a house. I wasn't eager to adopt any such plan. They wanted me to stay because I wasn't an easy worker to replace, but I needed to return to living my own life.

After my experience with the resistance in Brussels, I wasn't really keen on getting involved with it again, but I was becoming more interested in joining a regular army. I thought maybe I could join the British or American army before the war came to an end. The resistance also wasn't doing much militarily now that the Allies had arrived, and I wanted to hit the Germans where it counted, to go after them myself.

~

In September 1944, I said goodbye to Fexhe-le-Haut-Clocher and took the train to Brussels. So much new activity was now out in the open there: people were gathering in public places again and Zionists were starting to organize.

In Brussels, I felt free for the first time in many years. It was strange to be able to walk around anywhere without running into guards, check posts or mass arrests.

I went out to Strombeek-Bever to look for Dirk, the painter, and found him there. He told me that after the last time I'd seen him in early 1943 he'd hidden a number of Jews. He had been caught, arrested and sent to a concentration camp. He'd just been released and had arrived home not long before my return.

According to Dirk, I could get work with the British Army; its main supply centre in Europe was located in Brussels. Huge storage depots, most of which were used to store food, had been installed in the city. Dirk had worked there briefly and knew that labourers were being hired regularly.

I easily found a job at the depot. They served us a satisfying meal at noon, and the wages were high. With my earnings, I could now take care of myself adequately. Since I was used to hard work, I was able to carry heavy sacks and boxes all day long. We unloaded lorries that arrived from the coast and loaded others that were going to the front. It was a massive undertaking.

One Sunday I decided to ride out to Waterloo to see what was going on there. After an absence of over a year, I dropped in at the farm where I'd worked. The young wife and Fernand were out, but his miserly mother was there.

She seemed glad to see me and invited me to sit with her to have a cup of coffee. She told me what had happened in the year I'd been away, about the family and the people I'd worked with. Then she asked me to come back to work there! She promised to give me a room. I had just left a much better job than hers and was looking forward to a different kind of life altogether, so her offer didn't appeal to me.

In Brussels I was renting a pleasant room overlooking a beautiful garden — far more agreeable living arrangements than my previous ones — and was even able to save some money. My job at the depot, however, held no real challenge for me, so when I noticed that the American army was advertising for interpreters I presented myself at the army headquarters. After filling out an application and talking to an American officer, I was tested for language proficiency.

I didn't expect anything to materialize from this. And yet when I returned from work one evening, I found a message in my room informing me that someone had called requesting me to be at the American headquarters the next morning at ten o'clock, sharp. I'd already been tested for languages. In German and French, I was perfectly fluent. I spoke Dutch and English, too, though my English was less fluent at that time than I would like to think it is today.

At ten o'clock the next morning I appeared as requested. Immediately, I was led to an officer who asked, "Are you ready to join us?"

"Yes," I answered. "When?"

"Today," he said.

Jolted, I said, "Oh! Why..."

He charged ahead. "We don't have much time. There's a war on. We can't wait. Are you willing to attend a swearing-in ceremony this morning?"

I'd been waiting for this opportunity; I snatched it. "Okay," I nodded. "Sure."

"Go in right now," he ordered. "We'll swear you in."

The same day, I gave up my room and the few possessions I couldn't carry with me. Several hours later, I checked in and was issued a uniform.

I moved out of Brussels with the American army that afternoon.

Interpreting Home

Dispatched from Brussels, we arrived in Maastricht, of all places, that evening. The American army had taken over an old hotel near the railway station. I went to look around; I hadn't been in Maastricht since the middle of 1942.

There was no war damage in Maastricht. I walked to the district where my aunt and her family had lived: her house was intact, but it was occupied by strangers. I spoke to some neighbours and none of them could tell me anything about the Schmidts.

I stayed there a few days and used my spare time trying to find people I knew. I'd met many people there in the past.

On the second or third day while roaming around, I saw a familiar face on a balcony. It was Mr. Brunn and his wife, staring in my direction; they didn't seem to recognize me in my American uniform.

I called out, "Mr. Brunn, don't you recognize me?"

"Oh!" he said, "Moishe! It's you!"

"Yeah," I smiled. "It's me. What's happening here, Mr. Brunn? Where's my aunt and the others?"

"Ah," he stammered, "you know... your aunt and the children, your uncle, they all went away. They were taken away. They haven't come back."

The Brunns were Jews from Germany who had lived in the Netherlands a long time. They'd been fairly wealthy. They'd escaped deportation by hiding somewhere, but their two daughters had not been in hiding and had been arrested. My relatives, the Schmidts, and the two Brunn children were gone.

The Brunns told me about the roundup that took place in the Maastricht area. Jews were herded together and carted away. The elderly Brunns were among the few who were left.

I said to them, "Look, I have to go. We're moving out of Maastricht soon. But whenever I can, I'll come see you."

I did just that: whenever I had leave from the army, I went to spend time with them. Theirs was a hollow existence. Though they hoped at first that their daughters would return, they never did. The old people had lost everything. I became like a son to them. They looked forward to my visits and pampered me with all kinds of food and fuss.

After I joined the Americans, I found myself facing a sudden major counter-offensive by the Germans. In the middle of December, the Germans made a fast move across Belgium toward Antwerp. They tried to sever the British from the American troops by splitting through the centre of the Allied front. The action took place a short distance from our position.

During three days of dense fog, German paratroopers dropped from the skies. American soldiers didn't know who was who: they were calling to one another, thinking the Germans were standing right beside them. I was south of Maastricht at the time. My unit didn't know all the details, but we knew there was fighting very close to us.

Then the sun came out. The German push was cut off; the Battle of the Bulge was turning in our favour, though there would be more than a month of fighting before it was over. This was the only engagement in which my company was imperiled.

After that we travelled into Germany. I had never dreamed of ending up there. It was just by a stroke of luck in signing on as an interpreter that I was returning to Germany.

I experienced a strange feeling when I crossed the border in an American uniform. The crossing point was southeast of Maastricht, and fierce fighting was going on there. Planes and bombs were screaming around us.

For the first time, I saw German cities completely destroyed. The cities we drove through were endless rubble; there was almost nothing left. Walls had tumbled down. We had to be careful where we stepped.

My group would move into areas immediately after they had been bombed. We were sometimes the first ground force to push forward. There were always several soldiers with me whenever we were ordered to occupy any specific building. Even though the Germans were sometimes still shooting from the rooftops, I felt fearless and even recall running way ahead of the other guys.

Astounded, the soldiers with me asked, "How come you're running ahead of us? What do you think you're doing? Aren't you scared?"

I answered exultantly, "No! I'm not scared. I'm happy!" And I forged ahead even faster. They couldn't understand it.

Afterwards, they insisted on talking about my behaviour. Some of the guys were perceptive and intelligent; a few were college graduates. They continued to question me, "How come you're not scared?"

"Because I know you guys are scared," I answered. Several of the soldiers had suffered an emotional collapse.

"I am enjoying this war," I told them. "I've been longing for combat for years. I only wish I could fight! I haven't fought enough!"

I'd been suppressed for years. The Nazis had muzzled me; they had almost crushed me. Thinking of what they'd done to me made me ache to tear them apart.

I wanted to fight, to take revenge. I had to vent my rage.

We moved northward in Germany. We were on the west side of the Rhine River, and the German army had withdrawn over the river to the east side. I was stationed then in Krefeld, less than one hundred kilometres from Wattenscheid, but Wattenscheid was still in German hands. The Rhine divided the two sides, and artillery firing from both banks was ferocious.

My unit was billeted in a rich man's villa outside Krefeld. We discovered a large wine cellar full of bottles of choice German wine, which sparked the longest party of my life. We all shared the spoils. I drank six bottles of wine by myself. I was deliriously happy! I sang and played the fool — the happiest man in the world and utterly drunk. By the end of the party, I couldn't move without falling down.

We emptied the whole cellar to the last bottle. I was out of commission for at least three days, in a sodden haze. None of our group reported for duty. We were all wrecked for three days — officers and everyone. We were never reprimanded for any of this, and the incident stays in my mind as a celebration of the Nazi defeat. A hallelujah victory celebration.

We were still on the west side of the Rhine. The German batteries on the east side kept blasting across the river, destroying their own cities in order to hit us. I was kept well behind the front lines and was never involved in the battles. Sometimes, however, I had to go forward to investigate or interrogate someone. The army was taking German prisoners and some were high-ranking officers. We needed to pry information from them about German positions and the strength of their troops.

The questioning was conducted fairly, unlike what I'd experienced with the Gestapo. The captives were seated in a room, and we talked to them. I never saw any brutality.

Sometimes we captured an SS man trying to pass himself off as an ordinary soldier. Though I was only supposed to be the translator, in cases like these I participated in the questioning by bringing up points the Americans had not thought of. I was well aware of SS crimes.

The "Black Shirts," however, never gave a straight answer. They feigned innocence and denied everything. It was difficult to deal with them — I felt like taking a stick and beating them over the head, applying their own methods to them. The Americans wouldn't tolerate such tactics, so in some ways I felt under restraint. I had to sit and listen to the garbage they spewed out.

Interrogations of regular officers were much simpler; the Americans tried to deal with these on a soldier-to-soldier basis. Strategy and emplacements and military strength were what mainly interested them, as well as the civilian situation on the other side of the Rhine. The American army had to plan its advance into Germany so as to minimize the loss in human lives. The war was still being fought and, at that time, the Americans weren't much interested in probing into criminal responsibility.

The Americans made a distinction between the regular army and the SS, knowing that soldiers would ultimately be released after the fighting had ended, whereas the SS might be brought to trial; they therefore guarded the SS more securely. During interrogations, however, the distinction never came out because we had no witnesses or evidence against individual SS officers. Suspecting that a particular person had been a concentration camp guard wasn't proof, and we didn't have the mandate to pursue such suspicions. It was often exasperating.

Even after they had lost the west side of the Rhine, the Germans still believed they would win in the end. The prisoners we took were very defiant, and it was their defiance that annoyed me more than anything else. When it was obvious to the rest of the world that they were whipped, they still acted like they were the master race.

Often we captured young soldiers who were only fifteen or sixteen. They knew next to nothing but were fanatic Nazis. I was shocked by the fanaticism still rampant in Germany. I was horrified to find that belief in Hitler was stronger in 1945 than it had been when I had left seven years earlier. The Germans believed their government's propaganda that they had really won the war but had been betrayed by a mysterious force. They couldn't grasp that Hitler had lost the war, which seemed impossible to them.

While I was stationed in Krefeld, I met a German who identified himself to me as a Jew. He told me he'd been living in Krefeld with a German family. I don't know if it was true or not; he may have been a Nazi who chose hastily to call himself a Jew — a safe cover suddenly, whereas before the Allies had advanced across Europe it had been the greatest offence. I was disinclined to believe the man's story.

From Krefeld I moved south along the west side of the Rhine to Koblenz, then further south to Mainz. When we could finally cross the Rhine River, which was late March or early April 1945, I was posted in Würzburg.

The Allied armies moved in all directions across Germany. I was attached to the army in the south. My unit never came across any concentration camps. But we began to hear the horror stories. When the camps were liberated by Allied troops, photographs of the survivors and ghastly reports appeared in the world press. What went on in the camps became common knowledge. I wasn't surprised to hear about all the camps, but even I was shocked by the extremes to which the Nazis had gone. I'd known that many people would die under their heel — I hadn't imagined the numbers would be so great.

At the end of April 1945, we heard that Hitler had killed himself. We weren't sure if it was true, since there were also rumours contradicting this news. He had said he would fight from the mountains of Bavaria; we were close to that area and expected to have to keep on fighting. It was a time full of rumours and uncertainties, though we were confident that the war would end soon.

We read the American army newspaper, *Stars and Stripes*, eagerly every day. One day it was headlined: GERMANY QUITS.

The day before, on May 7, 1945, the Germans had signed the surrender simultaneously in Reims, France, and Berlin, Germany. War in Europe was over.

We all congratulated each other. The end of the war against such a threatening and powerful enemy was indeed a great occasion. The American soldiers were happy that they'd be able to return home. There were parties and festivities among us.

I stayed on in the army of occupation. The American sector was mainly in the south. The part of Germany where I came from was under British command. The French occupied the sector near Strasbourg, and the Soviets were in what would become known as East Germany.

With the war over, my unit became involved in civilian administration. I was an interpreter, often involved in investigating irregularities, crimes or disputes. The languages I used were German, English and occasionally French. The first time I encountered some French-Canadian soldiers, I guessed they were talking French but scarcely understood what they were saying. It sounded strange to me. When they switched, more or less, to European French, we communicated with each other more readily.

Each of the Allied armies had an engineering division that was rebuilding the railways in its sector. My unit was assigned to the railway system, usually at train stations, to help keep American supplies and personnel moving through the country.

A few times I thought of visiting Wattenscheid. The distance was under 350 kilometres, but transit lines were still disrupted. There was widespread wreckage, and the trains weren't running on schedule. Wattenscheid was also in the British zone, and it wasn't easy to travel between zones, which required special permission. I didn't expect to actually find anyone in Wattenscheid whom I particularly cared to see, so I didn't pursue it.

My plan was to go back to the Netherlands eventually. I'd been admitted there before the war with a valid visa; I could resume my interrupted journey from there to the Land of Israel. The Netherlands was liberated at the very end of the war, just a few days before Germany's complete surrender. Formidable combat had continued there much longer than in other areas, with Canadian troops fighting alongside the British. I couldn't travel to Amsterdam or Franeker until the war was over, and then it took months to repair the railways. I followed the progress through reports in newspapers.

The longer I stayed with the army, the more I felt it was a waste of time. There was nothing I could learn. It wasn't interesting. It was peacetime service, working a routine shift and eating huge meals.

Every variety of food was provided and we could eat as much as we wanted. It was all brought from the United States in cans and packages. The quality and quantity were much greater than had been available during the war. On my first morning in the army in Maastricht, I ate twelve eggs for breakfast. I hadn't eaten eggs for years — the farmers hadn't kept hens because they required too much feed. I got very sick as a result of my greed. Even afterwards when I ate less greedily, I suffered diarrhea for several weeks before adjusting to the rich diet. Meals became the best feature of life with the army.

I also learned fluent English — American army English, of course. The soldiers came from many parts of the United States — I even met a few Jews from New York and New Jersey — and told me all kinds of things about the country and life there. They talked about Black citizens. There were no Black soldiers in my outfit; they were segregated and served in different units.

I worked directly with the train system, the railway workers and passengers. Sometimes I spoke with survivors of concentration camps who came through on trains. They told me horrible stories about the camps.

I had free passes to travel on trains, so when I was occasionally given leave, I could travel. I managed to go back to Maastricht to visit the Brunns a few times. I had to travel from Würzburg, Germany, to Liège, where I changed trains for Maastricht. I had lived near Liège for a year but had never been there. When I finally got there, I could see it was large and sprawling and, no doubt, a fine city. Nevertheless, the only part I walked through was the station; I felt no attachment to the place.

On a visit to the Brunns one evening in mid-1945, I arrived in Maastricht late because the train had been delayed. At the door of the Brunns' house I met a girl searching for a key. I didn't know who she was. Finally, she found the key and unlocked the door. She knew about me from the Brunns and let me into the house. The Brunns were out.

I asked her who she was and heard her story. Her name was Shoshana, and she was living with the Brunns, who were trying to adopt her. She was a German-Jewish girl whose parents had been killed by the Nazis. She'd been hidden for several years by some miners in the district of Maastricht. She was eighteen years of age and engaged to marry a Jewish man who owned a small shop in Heerlen, an industrial city near Maastricht.

The Brunns returned home and we all sat down to a meal. I'd brought food from the army. I stayed at the Brunns for a number of days and sometimes talked with Shoshana, but she wasn't around very often.

~

I was paid regularly by the army and was issued two hundred cigarettes every week. I wasn't a smoker, so I sold the cigarettes. At long last, I was accumulating a sizable sum of money, but there was nowhere to spend it. Würzburg, for instance, was a city in ruins. Few buildings were standing. My unit was living in railway cars.

So I saved all my money. I couldn't deposit it anywhere, so I had to keep it on me. I kept it in my pocket or under my pillow, as I had while working on the farm in Waterloo. When I visited the Brunns, I left my savings with them.

When I was able to travel to Brussels, I decided to spend one of my breaks from the army with my friend Dirk. I stuffed my duffel bag with food and cigarettes, soap and razor blades — all kinds of scarce items. I wanted to bring these to repay his many kindnesses and his friendship toward me.

I went out to Strombeek-Bever and found him at home. His wife was there, too. They'd just become proud parents. Dirk was so happy to see me and gave me a warm welcome. I unpacked all the goodies

I'd brought, and he and his wife danced with delight. I spent a few glowing days with them.

I continued to visit the Brunns several times during the rest of 1945. Each visit, I spent time with Shoshana. She would ask me about the army and about Germany; she hadn't been out of a narrow neck of the Netherlands for many years and was curious about other places.

The Germans slowly took over the railway system after the Americans handed it back to them. We remained in charge of the railway workers and were still checking the trains, but I felt that I was frittering away my time. There wasn't much to do, and I actually hated being in Germany. I was full of resentment toward the nation.

One day a Jewish girl travelling from Frankfurt to Munich came to our office at the station to complain that she couldn't find a seat on the train. I told her I'd try to get her a seat and went with her into a first-class carriage. A German was sitting there, an arrogant man who looked to me like an SS-type. I could imagine him flicking a whip and lashing out at people. I couldn't bear the sight of the man.

I said to him, "Is this your seat?" I spoke to him in German. He didn't answer me. He pretended he didn't hear me, didn't see me.

I repeated, "Is this your seat?" No response.

I grabbed him by the coat. I demanded, "Is this your seat?" He answered, "Yes. Yes." Each word was like a gunshot. "Where's your ticket?" I persisted.

He showed me his ticket. I snapped, "Get up! Get up!" and I told the girl, "This is your seat now. You sit here."

I don't know if his ticket was for that seat; I didn't look at it. All I saw was a *fahrbissener* — a staunch, committed — Nazi. I said to him, "Come with me."

He sat motionless. He didn't budge. I pulled him up. I shoved him.

He was bigger than me, tall and solid, a heavyweight; I was no more than middleweight. But I had on an American uniform and I was seething with anger.

I pushed him forward. I drove him along the platform. He barely moved, so I shoved him like they used to shove me. I hit him in the ribs like they had hit me, like they had hit so many of us.

I ordered, "Go on. Faster. Move! Move! Faster! Faster!" I grew angrier by the minute.

He reached the top of the staircase leading down from the platform. Again he didn't move. I shoved him. Then I kicked him. I kicked him so hard that he rolled right down the stairs. He lay at the bottom and didn't get up. I walked away. I left him there. I paid no more attention to him.

Some Americans working in the station saw what happened and objected to my actions. "You're not supposed to do that," they said. "We're going to report you."

"I had to do that," I countered. "It's my job. The guy's a Nazi — he behaves and looks like a Nazi. I had to do that. You do what you want. If you want to report me, report me."

They reported me to a senior officer. They said that while I was on duty, I had hit a German passenger and thrown him down the stairs. I was summoned to the office of the major in command of our unit. "What happened?" the major demanded. "What were you doing?"

I replied, "Major, that was my revenge." He knew something about my experiences. He knew I'd been in the underground army.

"I had to do that," I explained. "I had to get it out of my system. Penalize me if you want to; do what you want."

"Forget it," he grumbled. "I haven't seen anything; I don't know anything. Just don't do it again."

Later the other soldiers told me they had taken the German to the hospital. His arms and three ribs were broken. I had really let go. I had to deal with Germans every day and I couldn't pay them back for what they'd done to me and others.

I never mixed with Germans. I kept to the American compound, where I could live in complete isolation. The army had its own supplies, its own canteen, American movies and entertainment.

The major commanding our unit wanted to recommend me for

the officers' training school and the regular army. He laid out the opportunities for me: "You can go to the United States. You can get an immigration visa and become an American citizen."

I enjoyed my association with the Americans. I found them refreshing compared to Europeans. But I wasn't interested in their enticements at the time. My plan was to go to Israel;[1] I had no other goal. After all that I'd been through, I was convinced that there wasn't a future for Jews anywhere but in Israel.

It seemed to me that even Americans didn't like Jews very much. I noticed that some American Jews were always looking over their shoulders to see if they'd said the right thing and done the right thing.

The army days grew longer and longer. I decided the time had come to resume my fitful journey to Israel. I resigned from the army.

---

1   Morris is referring to the area that was called British Mandate Palestine until the State of Israel was declared in 1948. The usage of the term here and in the following pages reflects the voice of the author at this time. See the glossary entry for British Mandate Palestine for more information.

Regaining Myself

Early in January 1946, I went to the Brunns' in Maastricht. I was back in civvies again. I asked Mr. Brunn for my money, and he told me that a few weeks earlier the Dutch police had searched the house hunting for black market goods and money. They'd rummaged everywhere, and they just missed finding my money by a hair's breadth. It was stashed among the linens.

I left Maastricht and took a train up north. The trains were running again, but travel was still slow and often interrupted; many bridges hadn't been rebuilt. I spent about two days getting to Franeker. I arrived and found that everything there looked the same. I took a room in a small hotel and went to the town hall the next morning.

In most Western European countries, residents are registered in the local city hall. This was the custom in the Netherlands, too. I presented myself to the town clerk. "My name is Moritz Schnitzer. I lived here in Franeker for two years until late 1941. I was registered in this office. I'm a Jew from Germany. I'm stateless. The Nazis took away my citizenship — you've heard what happened.

"I've lost all my papers because of the war. You know what happened during the war. We were all pushed from place to place. I lost my resident visa and my Dutch work permit, so now I need to establish my identity."

He stared at me. "What? What's this you're saying? Is what you're saying true?"

"Sure, it's true!" I answered. "Ask some other people." He was a young man. "Ask older people — they'll tell you it's true."

Dumbfounded, he answered, "All right. What's your name? I'll look it up in my files."

He scanned some files and returned about five minutes later holding a paper. "Moritz Schnitzer. Yes. You died in 1942." "What do you mean?" I exclaimed. "How could I have died in 1942? Don't you see me here? I'm here. It's 1946. I'm standing in front of you. I'm not dead!"

"It says you're dead. And it has the official stamp."

"I don't care if it's stamped or not," I protested. "I'm here right in front of you. How can I be dead?" I pointed at the document. "See the picture? It looks like me doesn't it?"

"Yeah," he agreed. "It looks like you."

"Then how can I be dead if I'm standing in front of you?"

He was stumped. "I don't know what we can do. I can't do anything about it. You're dead and that's that."

The death had been certified by someone in the local administration. The Germans had probably furnished a list naming people who were dead and no one had questioned it.

"Look, there has been a mistake. There has to be a solution."

He finally conceded. "I'll talk to the mayor."

The mayor was in his office when the clerk went up to consult him.

Soon the mayor came down and questioned me. "You're one of the Jewish boys who was here before?"

"Yes, I am."

"I see. That's very interesting," he said. Still hesitating he repeated, "Is this true what you're saying?"

"Certainly, it's true," I replied. "You can see my picture right there. I know this place. I've been here before. I'm no stranger to Franeker. I lived here for two years."

He relented. "Sit down for a few minutes." He searched through a law book and a code of regulations, then he said, "All right. If you can bring me a witness who'll testify that you are Moritz Schnitzer, then we'll fill out all the papers for you and give you an identification card."

My one recourse was to go to a farmer I'd worked for. Maybe the farmer would recognize me and be my witness.

I walked out of the building and along the main street. I passed the old train station we'd lived in; the structure was still there. I continued down the Harlingerweg toward the farm that used to be three minutes by bicycle from the hachshara.

A farm labourer saw me and recognized me right away! He gasped, "Ah, Mose!" They had called me "Mose" on that farm.

He came over and embraced me! Then he called the farmer.

The farmer, Van der Berg, came out. "Mose!" he cried. "You!" And he kissed me! There were tears in his eyes — a Friesian farmer crying! I had always thought those people had no emotions. My unexpected return had fractured a deep reserve.

The next thing the farmer did was take me into his living room. I had never seen the living room before, as I had always been in the stable.

He sat me down in the kitchen. "You must eat with us."

His two sons, who had worked with me, also remembered me, as did his wife. What a simcha, celebration, it was! An unbelievable reception.

Van der Berg kept saying, "I'm so happy to see you and that you're alive! I'm so happy! We talked about you all the time. We wondered what had happened to all the boys and girls... what had happened to all of you. It has been so long... so many years with no news. People said that all of you died and now you're here."

These people were religious. To them, it was as if I'd come back from the dead. They were awed to see me alive.

The farmer himself offered to accompany me to the town hall. He said immediately, "I'll take my bike. You take my son's bike." And away we went.

We entered the town hall and the office of the mayor. Van der Berg declared, "Of course Mose is Mose! I know him! Sure! It's true what he says!" And then he signed affidavits as my witness, clearing the past detritus from my life.

After fleeing the Gestapo so many years ago, I had finally received my own true identification card again. I thanked Van der Berg and said goodbye to him. I was leaving Franeker and going to Amsterdam. I could be my own self again.

~

I had to wait around for the day's one train. The Germans had seized many railway cars and taken them to Germany. Few passenger cars were available at that time, so we had to travel under primitive conditions in freight cars. At last, a couple of days later, I reached Amsterdam — *Mokum*, the place, as the Friesians called the city.

I thought it would now be simple to obtain ration tickets, which were still in use even for basic foods. Also, I needed an updated visa to stay in the Netherlands.

I went to the city hall in Amsterdam and learned that I would have to see the police before being issued these papers. "Many war criminals are sneaking in here. We can't give out anything before you get clearance."

I hurried to the police station. Three or four people were ahead of me. They were under great strain. When my turn arrived, I told the police officer who I was and that I'd been on hachshara in the Netherlands until the end of 1941. I added a few more facts.

The police officer observed, "You are Yehudi" (a Jew).

I replied, "Yes, of course. You know what we went through, all of us."

He nodded. "Sure," and gave me the necessary clearance.

"You're kosher now," he remarked. He happened to also be Jewish!

I walked out with my clearance papers and returned to the city hall. I'd had a visa before the war, and now it was renewed. I was a legal resident of the Netherlands again.

By January 1946, the Mizrachi organization was running a residence called a *Beth Chalutz*, a pioneer house, in Amsterdam for people who were planning to settle in the Land of Israel. Founded by
men who'd been in the Jewish Brigade of the British Army, the residence had sleeping and eating accommodations for displaced people,
so I stayed there on my return to Amsterdam.

Meanwhile, the Zionist group I'd been affiliated with was about to
set up a new hachshara in Dieren near Arnhem. It had been started
from scratch about two weeks after I arrived in Amsterdam, because
people like me were now surfacing after so many years of war.

The only other person to reappear from our original group that
had been located in Franeker was Bram, the Dutch fellow who'd escaped with me in November 1941. After he and I had split up, he'd
succeeded in crossing over to England. There he'd joined the Free
Dutch Forces.

Things balance out in strange ways. In 1941, I had probably saved
Bram's life. Then after the war, he was the source of a momentous turn
in my life. I met him in Amsterdam in January 1946. Through him,
my brother Eddi subsequently learned that I was alive, because Bram
mentioned me to a friend of his in England who knew my brother,
and that person told Eddi about me.

I was in residence in Amsterdam when I received a telegram from
Eddi. It came from Canada and read:

OVERJOYED TO HEAR YOU ARE ALIVE. I AM OK. CABLE
ANSWER ABOUT EVERYTHING. WILL SEND PARCELS, MON-
EY. WIFE AND I WILL SEE YOU HERE SOON.
    LOVE,
    EDMUND

I cabled an answer immediately to let him know I'd received the telegram. He wrote me by airmail the same day outlining details of his
past five years and formulating plans. His cable and letter were dated
February 5, 1946, one day after my twenty-fourth birthday.

~

I moved to the hachshara in Dieren a few days later and wrote back to Eddi from there. I wasn't thinking seriously about his proposal to go to Canada, as I was still set on going to Israel.

I was the only survivor of Franeker to participate in the new hachshara. Bram didn't rejoin because he was still unwell after contracting tuberculosis during the war. Since I had been on hachshara before, the organizers put me in charge. I was the most experienced person there.

In Dieren, I now gave the religious lessons, just as Rabbi Yehoshua Wolf had wanted me to do years earlier. I performed all the functions that Rabbi Wolf had performed in Franeker.

We built a busy hachshara. We had between twenty-five and thirty members, most of us working on farms as we'd done in Franeker. This time, however, we sent some members to learn trades. I myself went back to farming — by now it was easy for me. I enjoyed it, too, and found the work satisfying compared to working in an army of occupation. Some of us worked on contract, as was common in Belgium during the sugar-beet season. Teams of us took on specialized jobs for farmers. We worked very hard.

We also enrolled in a study program at a local agricultural school. In response to our request for instruction in theoretical farming, the principal gave us an initial course on the chemistry of soils and fertilizers. I surprised myself by picking it up very fast even though I hadn't studied much chemistry before. At the Adath Israel *Gymnasium* in Berlin I'd done a little science but eight years later I had forgotten all of it.

I memorized every formula our instructor wrote down, quickly and accurately. He said to me one day, "In all the years that I've been teaching, I've never had a student who grasped a subject as fast as you do."

I took several more of his courses and he got to know me well.

Then he said to me, "I'd like to send you to the agricultural university in Wageningen. I want to sponsor you."

He was mentally stimulated by teaching our eager group and appreciated my ability to quickly learn the material. Usually he taught uninterested farm boys and couldn't drive anything into their heads. To my astonishment, he offered me a college education at his own expense.

Our courses were given in the evenings because of our daytime work. I was attending a class one day when someone came to fetch me. "There's a phone call for you from Canada."

We didn't have a phone in the hachshara, so I went to take the call in a hotel. Eddi was on the line with his father-in-law. "We're glad you survived the war, Moishe," his father-in-law said. "Now we want you to come to Canada."

I told him, "Thanks for the invitation but I want to go to Israel. I've been preparing myself to go for seven years, since 1939. That's why I'm here on hachshara…"

I had started the hachshara and was now in charge of it. I couldn't leave the group. I explained this to Eddi and his father-in-law.

Afterwards, just as they had at the start of the war, the British blockaded British Mandate Palestine. Legal immigration had become impossible. The only way to enter was covertly on what was called Aliyah Bet, a movement that attempted to circumvent the blockade. Some Jews who tried this dangerous method lost their lives in the attempt. Most who came from displaced persons camps in Europe were turned back and interned by the British in Cyprus and elsewhere, often detained for months.

I continued writing to my brother while still planning to go to Israel. I was helping build an active organization in the Netherlands. We now had several hundred members.

Then who arrived in Dieren? Unexpectedly, Shoshana. She suddenly appeared and wanted to join the kibbutz.

"I thought you were going to marry a man from Heerlen — I thought you were engaged to him!" She had always given me the impression that she would be married soon.

"I was engaged to marry him, yes, but I couldn't go through with it. I didn't like him that much."

She became a member of the hachshara in Dieren; she left Maastricht and moved in with us. We saw more and more of each other, and I fell in love with her. And she with me. I'd impressed her as an experienced person; I'd knocked around. The other man was settled in Heerlen, a not too exciting life.

Shoshana was a talented artist, a potter. She was attractive, with black hair and big brown eyes. After a while, I asked her to marry me.

She was under twenty-one and a ward of the state: after the war, the Dutch authorities had begun to take an interest in orphaned Jewish children because of pressure from the churches. The Protestant Church, for example, had been trying to convert some children who'd been saved by church members during the war. The state therefore assumed guardianship of these children.

To marry Shoshana, I needed permission from the state. So I went to the Ministry of Social Welfare in Amsterdam and explained my situation to the officials. They made all kinds of objections, primarily that I had no income and wasn't settled. As the ones responsible for deciding what was in her best interests, they refused permission for the marriage.

I told Shoshana, "We can't get married here but we'll be leaving the Netherlands; the government will have no jurisdiction over you then. We'll get married in France on our way to Israel. It isn't much of a problem."

Everyone in the kibbutz knew our plans; we spent all our spare time together. Whenever I was called to Amsterdam to work in our head office, she was painfully lonely. I'd become secretary of Bachad, the Young Mizrachi of the Netherlands; I was the senior member of the organization for a time. We had a group of fifty or sixty members in Amsterdam. I devoted considerable energy to organizing the group.

In Amsterdam I always stayed in a hostel called the Joodse Invalide. Jewish people of all ages lived there. It was the only public place in the city to get kosher food. I met my distant cousin Avram Heller there. He was the younger brother of Moishe Heller, who'd been with me on hachshara in Franeker.

Avram's father and mother had survived the war and were staying at the hostel. Avram had come from his kibbutz in Palestine to be with them; at the same time, he was acting as *shaliach*, envoy, for the HaKibbutz HaDati movement, a branch of the Bachad. He spent about a year in the Netherlands. Avram and I worked side by side in the Mizrachi organization. Since I was familiar with Dutch conditions and he was a first-rate organizer, he advised me on what should be done and helped me carry out programs.

I met hardly any Jews I'd known before. I tried to find the Kosters in Amsterdam and was told that, a few months after I'd left his home, Professor Koster had been arrested, on the grounds that he wasn't wearing a yellow star. The only one of his family to survive the war was the child who'd had special needs and had been placed in a non-Jewish home.

I had tried to locate members of my family when I first reached Amsterdam in 1946. I haunted the refugee agencies and checked every register. Jewish groups such as the World Zionist Organization, as well as the Red Cross and the United Nations Relief and Rehabilitation Administration (UNRRA), were actively tracing and resettling people. These organizations published lists of survivors and tried to locate relatives, which was a massive international effort. My parents' and Benno's names never emerged.

I continued my search for many years. I pursue this information to this day.

Eddi, too, made inquiries through Canadian, American and British organizations. We tried to locate anyone we'd known who was missing.

When reports described how the Nazis had killed six million Jews, I was still optimistic that Benno, at least, had survived. He had youth and strength to his advantage. But slowly I accepted the fact that Eddi and I were probably the only ones alive in our immediate family. My parents, my brother Benno, my paternal grandmother, the Schmidts, the Brunn girls, the group in Franeker, Piefke Levy and many others had disappeared.

~

Passover 1946 arrived. After the holiday, the entire group on hachshara was planning to move down to Marseille, France, to board a boat for Israel. I spent Passover in Maastricht with the Brunns. Shoshana was there, too.

The holiday was interrupted by a call from our head office asking me to come to Amsterdam immediately. I hurried there and found our leaders assembled, Avram Heller among them. They enjoined on me to wait in the Netherlands and not rush to Marseille, warning me that I would get stuck in Marseille for some time. I would be more useful to the movement if I remained in the Netherlands.

I returned to Maastricht and reported this to Shoshana. She exploded with anger, accusing me of delaying and betraying her, of renouncing the marriage. Fuming, she alleged that my refusal to go to France after Passover was because I didn't want to marry her.

I tried to explain that I had no authority, that none of our group could go to Marseille, that she wasn't free to go either. But she misconstrued the situation and railed that it was all my doing — that I'd manipulated the council into postponing our departure. Then she broke off our engagement.

She was blaming me when, in fact, political events had militated against our going. What hurt me most was her urging me to go with her to France, as previously planned, despite the council's decision. She refused to understand that it would have been rash to do so.

We both stayed at the hachshara. That summer I became more involved with running the head office and organizing the Amsterdam group, so I took a room at the Joodse Invalide for a few months.

The year was drifting by. A symphony orchestra formed in Arnhem, a city near Dieren, and concerts began. Some members of the hachshara were musically trained, so in the fall of 1946, the group decided to attend a series of concerts. There was a concert every month, and I became fond of classical music.

The Concertgebouw Orchestra had given concerts when I lived in Amsterdam in 1941 and 1942. The Kosters attended those concerts, but I never could because I had to avoid all public gatherings. After the war, however, I heard the Concertgebouw Orchestra in its concert hall in Amsterdam.

Whenever I went to Dieren, I saw Shoshana. I still cared for her very much and she seemed to feel something for me, too, but we kept our distance.

Our organization continued to hold us back, delaying everything. The leaders declared that a chance to leave would come before long. "Don't move," they said. "The border to Israel will open one day soon. Stay put for now."

My brother continued to write to me regularly, repeating, "Come to Canada. You can study here. You were always a good student. If you come, you'll be able to develop yourself, do what you want to do. If you go to a kibbutz in Israel, you'll never be able to study."

By then, in my twenty-fifth year, I knew that if I didn't go back to school soon, I never would. I'd never yet seen the outside of a university, let alone the inside. And I'd always dreamed of studying something, of being somebody someday. Here I was. After twenty-five years, my greatest achievement was surviving the war.

Eddi dangled the bait before me. He asserted, "You have an obligation to educate yourself. You haven't done so yet, because you didn't have the opportunity. Come to Canada. You'll have the opportunity."

After a while I began to think, *Here I am, sitting in the Netherlands. I can't go to Israel. I'm bogged down in nowhere land. I have wasted my time in jails, then with the army. Now I'm in the same fix again.*

Our leaders counselled, "Be patient. Run the hachshara until we're ready to move." They hesitated to risk having too many people interned by the British. It was a very trying period.

Early in 1947, I discussed the situation with Avram Heller. I put all the facts to him and asked him, "What should I do?" He knew my whole history. Now I underlined the point that I had a chance to study.

Avram agreed with Eddi's opinion. "If you go to Israel, you'll end up in a kibbutz. You'll have no chance to study. Now you have a chance — go!"

He himself had lived in a kibbutz in the Land of Israel since about 1936. "If you have a chance to study," he said, "study. Then come to Israel after you've finished."

This was the compromise he proposed. This was the solution.

I was leaning in that direction of my own accord. I'd been coming to the conclusion that my life had been miserable enough. As I had a chance to educate myself, I thought I should do so. And Avram helped me reach that decision.

When I announced my plan, Shoshana heard about it and confronted me again. She told me not to go to Canada. She was afraid that if I went she would never see me again. She wanted me to go to Israel, as she still was planning to do. She suggested we should marry, as we had planned before.

By now I was wary of Shoshana. I told her that if we still felt strongly about each other later on and if it was materially possible, I would try to bring her to Canada. This didn't satisfy or convince her. I had now realized I couldn't take Shoshana with me. My brother was living with his in-laws and could only accommodate one person. He couldn't look after a couple, which would be too heavy a burden on him. I'd also often seen her moody and sensed it would be difficult for me to deal with her. She tended to put pressure on me impulsively. So even though we had become close again and she urged me not to go, to stay with her, I was determined to go.

On the Way to Canada

Eddi obtained a Canadian visa for me. Near the end of January 1947, he wrote to tell me the visa was on its way by surface mail and would reach The Hague in two months. I was then to present myself to the Canadian embassy in The Hague. I needed an additional travel document. I had only the identification card I'd obtained in Franeker, so I went to the Dutch police and requested a document that would permit me to travel. They refused to give it to me. "You're not Dutch," they explained.

"Then how can I travel?" I demanded. "I'm stateless. But I have a chance to go to Canada — and then you'll be rid of me."

Whenever I'd applied for an extension of my visa, I'd been given the runaround: the police had conveyed clearly that I wasn't welcome. Now I flung at them, "I'm not welcome here, so why don't you give me a chance to leave? Give me a travel document and I'll leave. You won't have to deal with me anymore."

They wouldn't do it. They refused to do anything to help me.

In March, I finally went to the Foreign Office in The Hague. I told the officials there, "I'd like to get a document so I can leave the country. I don't want to stay here any longer. I'm disgusted with this country."

I was blunt and brutally frank. "You don't want me. I don't want you. So give me a travel document. Then I can go." About a week later they sent me an identity certificate for use by aliens travelling from the Netherlands to other countries.

In April, I presented myself at the Canadian embassy. The prospective immigrants there were all women, war brides who wanted to join their husbands in Canada. I was the only man. Very few displaced people were immigrating so soon after the war. In fact, as odd as it sounds, Canada still had no Minister of Immigration, since the Immigration Branch was part of the Department of Mines and Resources!

I spoke to the visa officer, who told me that I needed to have a medical checkup. After the checkup, I went back to him, and after examining the chart he said, "Everything is okay."

He was about to stamp the visa in my travel document when he recalled, "You have to buy a ticket before I can give you the visa. You need a boat or airplane ticket for Canada, then come back for the visa."

I quickly headed to the KLM airline office and what *tsuris*, trouble, I had there! No one would sell me a ticket. "How come you won't sell me a ticket?" I asked. "I have a visa waiting for me."

I also told Royal Dutch Airline officials that I wanted to get out of the Netherlands, that they could get rid of me. That tactic often worked for some reason, and they sold me a ticket, which I paid for with the money I'd saved while I was with the American army. The ticket was very expensive: it cost about one thousand dollars for a one-way fare from Amsterdam to Montreal.

The Canadian official then stamped the immigrant visa into my travel document. I was ready to go.

Before going on to Canada, I intended to visit relatives in England. The British embassy in The Hague granted me a temporary visa for the United Kingdom.

At that time, overseas flights couldn't land in Montreal, so I first had to fly to New York. The American consulate in Amsterdam gave me the required transit permit.

In my last few days in the Netherlands, I went to visit the Brunns. On my last day, I visited Shoshana, who was then in Amsterdam. I said goodbye to the three people who had been closest to me in the Netherlands.

On May 1, 1947, I left Amsterdam and flew to London in a small plane. Even when I arrived in London, I had some difficulty. I was detained at Croydon Airport by the British police. My cousin was waiting for me while the police held me back for over an hour. I don't know why I was held, but perhaps it was because I was travelling on an unusual document, or maybe they were checking my identity against lists of war criminals.

I had difficulty at every stop because of my irregular document. Fundamentally, the problem was that I'd been born in Germany. This hampered me during the war — I could never admit to my birthplace — and now, even after the war, it was still tripping me up. I was finally allowed through to see my relatives, whom I hadn't seen since 1937 when they had left their home in Dortmund, Germany.

A few days later I continued on my way. I took the train from Euston railway station in London to Glasgow, Scotland. From Glasgow, I went by bus to Prestwick where the flights for New York took off.

On May 6, I flew from Prestwick to Iceland, from Iceland to Newfoundland, and from Newfoundland to New York. When I landed in New York, I was led aside. There was an outbreak of a disease of some sort in London, and since I'd come through there I had to be inoculated. I was hurried away to be given a needle. My brother stood waiting, bewildered when I didn't walk out!

Then I had to pass through customs. I wasn't carrying much baggage, but I had to line up like everyone else.

Eddi saw me then. He sneaked in between the customs inspectors and came to my side. He was unbelievably happy! An emotional moment, seeing him again! I hadn't seen him for nine long years, not since 1938. He looked well — much better than I did. I had been on the road from London for about two days and I hadn't shaved. Eddi took me to a barbershop for a shave and a haircut. Then we boarded a plane to Montreal.

We arrived in Montreal, and my travel document was stamped "Landed Immigrant, Montreal Dorval Airport, May 7, 1947."

Epilogue

In June 1981, my wife, Leah, and I flew to Europe. I wanted to show her the area where I was born and also the places and jails I had inhabited during the war.

Forty-three years after I had left my hometown, Leah and I returned to Wattenscheid. We arrived by car, and I couldn't recognize a thing. After we parked the car and walked around and I was able to pick out two landmarks, the Catholic and Evangelical churches, everything fell into place.

The coal mines were closed, and instead of the slag heaps and grime, the streets were now immaculately clean, the buildings freshly painted, the environment green and apparently free of pollution. Our home and main store were gone, leaving nothing in their place but a large empty lot, which becomes the outdoor market square one day a week and otherwise provides parking for cars and bicycles for the adjoining business district, now a pedestrian shopping mall. A tall new department store now stood at the limit of what had once been our property, but the name emblazoned on the structure was not Hermann Schnitzer. Similarly, our former shoe store on the Oststrasse was tenanted now by a store with a different name. However, the large Woolworth store that had been there when I was growing up was still there. And some of the buildings around the "old market" square — our home — were designated heritage sites. One of these was the

Schulte Apotheke, which still housed the pharmacy plus the office and home of Dr. Robert Schulte, my boyhood neighbour and friend.

Robert greeted us at his door with quick recognition and warmth and swept us into his home to meet and sit down with his family. He telephoned the Schrocks: Erwin had recently died, to my great regret, but Hedwig was still as sweet and good and beautiful as ever. She and another employee of my parents — a woman who had had a boyfriend in the SS — had saved pictures of my family and loaned them to us to make copies for Eddi and me. Hedwig told me of my mother's courage in venturing out of the Jewish house in Dortmund by covering the Jewish star with a fur neckpiece; my father's retention of his dignity by always being impeccably dressed; and Benno's tears and concern for my parents in spite of his own exhaustion.

From Bochum with its mixture of sad reminiscences, heartwarming encounters, came an unanswerable silent question: *Why? How could it have happened?*

We visited several spas. Some, such as Bad Kreuznach, have essentially disappeared into the encroaching industrial area; others, such as Bad Neuenahr or Schlangenbad, are as pristine and perfect as they ever were.

We drove to the Netherlands next and looked for the camp that had swallowed up my friends. Poorly marked roads in a desolate region eventually led to a nature preserve frequented by happy cyclists and hikers. Buried within an unwholesome-looking swamp was a simple unadorned memorial: a glass case displays a model of Westerbork camp and a short piece of rail symbolizes the many transports that carried nearly 100,000 Jews, mainly Dutch citizens, from there to Auschwitz and other death camps. It took decades before a memorial was constructed. Perhaps the Dutch had preferred not to draw attention to a camp that they themselves had set up in 1939 to intern Jewish refugees from Germany and which the Nazi conquerors later took over, ready-made for their diabolical purposes.

The city of Franeker was next on this odyssey. It was unchanged, still picturesque. The old railway station building, site of the hachsha-ra, had been modernized with new windows and doors and was now a private home. The Van der Berg farm and the other farms I knew in the region were still operating family farms. And our next stop, at the former Zuiderzee, the beautiful old sailing port of Hoorn was still maintaining the island prison where I was jailed in 1940 by the Dutch and from which I was released a few days later, courtesy of the German army.

Amsterdam had by now almost obliterated its ancient Jewish quarter; Jewish life as it existed there in the 1930s had disappeared. The magnificent historical structure of the Portuguese Synagogue is a solitary relic. As in so many other European cities, the streets of Amsterdam are essentially *judenfrei,* free of Jews.

A Swiss colleague, Jean Neyroud, tried to unearth the document I was forced to sign in 1942, which ordered my expulsion from Swit-zerland, but he was told that such documents had all been destroyed. Were they destroyed? Or are the Swiss authorities reluctant to pub-licize what they did during the war years? The question nags me, es-pecially since my colleague was warned that I could be arrested even now if I returned to Switzerland because I had entered illegally in 1942. Nevertheless, I returned to Switzerland in 1981 at the invitation of the Chemical Society of Bern and later at the request of Swiss tele-vision to recount my wartime experiences. In La Chaux-de-Fonds, we quickly spotted the ineradicable image, the cantonal jail, though it has been enlarged with a new wing since the fateful day I spent there in 1942.

From La Chaux-de-Fonds we drove toward the Doubs River in heavy rain and mist. The road was narrow and sparsely travelled with steep cliffs on both sides of the river, which flowed violently. The whole area was thickly wooded and still not much developed. Where one crosses into France at Fournet-Blancheroche, the church in the little village square still dominated the heights, and I silently recalled the old priest who thought that Piefke and I were angels.

At Besançon, we visited the cathedral and the archbishop's palace. Then, after careful perusal of a city map, we found the awesome prison fronting on a deceptively quiet road. In Arbois, too — the town of Louis Pasteur — we located the church, now a museum, and, close by, the quiet street flanked by a high jail wall.

In Dijon, we visited the railway station from which I was shipped as a prisoner to Belgium. In Brussels, we tramped through much of the city, including the seedy area near the Gare du Nord and along the Rue Verte, which was still a red-light district. The prison at Saint-Gilles, which we didn't revisit, was reportedly still functioning. And Waterloo had become a busy suburb of Brussels; Fernand's farm was no longer there.

Then we drove to Fexhe-le-Haut-Clocher. It's still isolated — the main highway passes a few kilometres north of it. We easily found the Roberti farm, but it was no longer in use. The buildings were deserted and rundown, windows were broken and weeds were growing in the farmyard. An old caretaker told us that the farm was being put up for auction for a housing development.

Curiosity finally took us to Wavre, where I had had to pretend, as Jan Van Capelle, to be from. It proved to be a busy industrial city south of Brussels. In the main square stood an eloquent memorial to the martyrs of the resistance, which showed that the city's citizens had been active in fighting the Nazi occupation. Since my Belgian identity card was issued in Wavre, we checked the city map in the display case outside the city hall, and, yes, there is a Chaussée de Bruxelles. In the telephone directory, we found several listings for the name Van Capelle. Coincidence? Or a miracle? Perhaps my passion for football was not so trivial after all — it gave me Jan Van Capelle and, with him, guardian angels in the city of Wavre, Dirk the painter and last but certainly not least, the old farmer Monsieur Degive.

～

In March of 1999, after twenty-five years of repeated enquiries, my colleague Jean Neyroud managed to secure an extract of the 1942 record from the prison of La Chaux-de-Fonds. It stated that M. Schmitzer (my name misspelled in the official records), prisoner No. 249, a person of the Jewish religion or believed to be so, had been "Weggewiesen an die französische Grenze" (Expelled to the French border) on August 28, 1942. Thus, fifty-seven years after throwing me to the Germans the Swiss police confirmed this event without an apology.

Afterword

My father had a very long and successful life in Canada after his arrival in 1947. The determination and intelligence evident in his memoir served him well in quickly remaking his life once given the opportunity. As his brother Eddi had promised, he was soon able to go on to study at university. He spent his first summer in Canada secluded in the country house of Eddi's in-laws in the Laurentian Mountains north of Montreal, preparing to take the entrance exams, and was accepted at McGill University in the fall of that same year. During that first year, he spent all his free time with Eddi and his family: Eddi's Canadian wife, Fay, and their first son, Howard, who was born that year, as well as the grandparents. They were all very welcoming and supportive, and my father embraced this new family.

From the moment he was able to attend university, he did not stop. After earning a bachelor of science in chemistry, he went straight to his master's degree, then completed his PhD in 1955. He was always grateful to a young professor of first year chemistry at MacDonald College at McGill, where he was enrolled in a BSc with a major in engineering. This professor, just a few years older than my father at the time, took him aside one day and asked about his background and education. He told my father he should specialize in chemistry, since he seemed to have a natural inclination for the subject: he hardly took notes and got very high marks on tests. It was evident from the start that he took to the subject! Unfortunately, he did not remember the name of that young professor but was always grateful for that advice and encouragement.

In the summer of 1948, he met my mother, Leah Paltiel, when they were both working as counsellors at a camp in the Laurentians. They had a whirlwind courtship and married in September of that same year. She was studying French and then library science at McGill. They often spoke French together and sang romantic French songs by artists like Maurice Chevalier. I witnessed this bond years later when they would visit me in Spain, and after a few glasses of good wine, they would break into those charming old songs. It is my fondest memory of them as a couple.

On completing his doctorate, my father worked for two years as a research chemist in industry but soon landed a position on the Central Experimental Farm, part of the federal Department of Agriculture — which became Agriculture and Agri-Food Canada — in Ottawa, where he was a principal researcher until his formal retirement in 1991. In fact, however, he worked well beyond that time, continuing to go into his lab until past his ninetieth birthday. His mind was still clear until months before his death at the age of ninety-eight this spring, 2020, but his deteriorating eyesight did not allow him to continue to carry out research, write or edit papers. He wrote some four hundred scientific papers over his long career; I always remember him writing away madly by hand at the dining room table, which was essentially his desk at home. He also contributed to scientific textbooks and collections, and directed the research of some twenty-five postdoctoral fellows and visiting scientists from many different countries, something he particularly enjoyed. He was appreciated as a generous, clear and patient teacher. His parents would have been extremely proud of how much he made of the opportunities he encountered after the war. He was a member of numerous scientific societies in Canada and abroad, but his greatest honour was being awarded the Wolf Prize in Agriculture in Israel in 1996 for his pioneering work studying soil organic matter. It was a very moving ceremony in the Knesset in Jerusalem, surrounded by the beautiful Chagall stained-glass windows. My son and I were there with him, though sadly my mother had died several years before.

My father also came to be much appreciated as a speaker on topics other than soil chemistry, especially on the subject of the Holocaust and his own experiences during the war, or on themes from the Jewish studies he had undertaken with groups of friends interested in expanding and deepening their knowledge. Most recently, he spoke at the Montreal Holocaust Museum on the anniversary of Kristallnacht in November of 2019. At the age of ninety-seven, he spoke without notes, clearly and steadily, telling his own story of that period and of the final warning he received from his father that steeled his determination to resist and survive through the worst circumstances, always avoiding any cooperation with the Nazis. At the end of his talk, he strongly denounced what he felt was the general lack of resistance on the part of Jews in particular, and passionately urged us all to always keep fighting against oppression. His talk was very well received and many audience members, young and old, came to shake his hand afterwards.

I grew up with these stories, the stories of my father's childhood in Germany and his lost youth during the war. His misadventures in ice-cold Friesian ditches at dawn or with ice-cold Friesian farmers could make me weep with laughter. In fact, there was often some comic relief in the way he talked about his physical hardships, his encounters with authorities or his narrow escapes. I always thought his ability to keep on seeing the absurdity, the upside-down madness of his situation, kept him going as much as did his recognition of the everyday realities to be faced. Somewhere in his mind, no matter what role or what situation he was in at the time, there was always the original Moritz Schnitzer, not only monitoring his performance but also standing outside the madness — at least, I believe there must have been, because somehow he emerged intact.

The young man who emerged from this maelstrom had somehow managed to hold on to not only his physical self and his intelligence but also his essential humanity. He was not bitter, not twisted into hatred by his experiences, though he might be aghast, woeful, outraged, contemptuous. He blamed the people who did nothing, who went along, who betrayed, who took part; there was never any excuse for selling your soul, for losing your humanity. Thanks to these stories and the success I knew he made of himself, I grew up with a strong belief in the human spirit as well as a strong connection with other horrible stories we hear all the time, stories of oppression and suffering.

I can't be sure of all the lessons my father expected me to draw from his stories; I'm sure he knew I'd draw my own no matter what he intended. I learned the simple fact that even in the most so-called civilized of societies, circumstances can turn sour and be exploited by powermongers and madmen, and ordinary people can turn against each other thinking that they have something to gain. I learned that, yes, the truth is that in order to protect ourselves and safeguard our rights to our beliefs and practices, we must stand by everyone else's rights as well. There is no way out of it; we are condemned to coexist; we are interdependent. We must look out for each other.

I am especially grateful that he shared with me the stories of my murdered, lost family, so they could be part of me, too: my grandparents, Hermann and Rosa, and my red-headed uncle, Benno. When I first got to know them in my childhood, I wanted to know what they were like, and I tried to bring them to life in my imagination, through my father's anecdotes and descriptions. It was only much later, in my thirties, with a red-headed son of my own, that I would be suddenly and repeatedly overwhelmed by grief. The thought of those parents, dignified and hard-working people who had once believed they lived in the greatest country in the world, herded into ghettos and then cattle cars and Nazi camps with their youngest son; the thought of Benno, a teenage boy seeing his world collapse into madness, barely having lived any happy moments in his short life; and my grandmother, who hadn't been able to part with him, how she must have suffered as she saw his life slowly strangled away. I grieved their loss along with my father.

Since those early years, I've lived in many different places and at one time taught newcomers to Canada, many of them members of persecuted minorities like my father. Most of them were also similar to him in that they were well-educated and well-rounded and also very ambitious, just as my father was when he finally managed to get to Canada. They often had that wry sense of humour that helped keep them going, too. Occasionally they told me stories of their own that I rushed to tell my father, to unburden myself to someone who knew and to let him know that I continued to be aware of the whole spectrum of human possibilities. And I told my students, those new storytellers, that we must all make the best of what we have here and never be led into that downward spiral from prejudice to persecution. But in fact, they tended to know that better than most Canadians, I found.

My father's story, after all, is also one of many refugee stories, and it can be hard for many people to read. We are lucky to live these lessons second-hand, to only hear the stories of one of the darkest periods of history, when there were factories of death in the middle of Europe. My father's story makes us proud to be human but also ashamed. It reminds us of how people both betrayed and defended their essential humanity in a time so close to our own and in places supposedly so much like our own. It brings us closer to the nightly news on television, where we can always find stories like these. It gives an example of incredible levelheadedness, ingenuity, determination and integrity. It will, I hope, put your own life into perspective for some time to come.

My parents were together until my mother's death from cancer in 1994. My father supported and helped nurse my mother through her long, painful illness and enabled her to die at home. After her death, he was alone for a long time, but he maintained friendships and also participated regularly in the services and discussions of the small egalitarian Conservative synagogue that he and my mother had helped found years ago, where everyone, male and female, can take part in leading the service. He had another family, consisting of me, his daughter, my son, Jan, and his wife, Nadine, and their three small children. He also kept in touch with some of his cousins who had gone to Israel, especially Nahum Vered, who called him regularly and visited whenever he could. My father felt very close to these three generations that followed him, and we will always be so very fond and proud of him. He was a huge, strong but humble presence and I feel his absence deeply. He had much to teach us all, and I am glad that, through this book, his life lessons will continue to provoke thoughtful discussion on a wider scale.

Eve Schnitzer
July 2020

Glossary

Agudath Israel (Hebrew; Union of Israel) An Orthodox political organization established in 1912 in Poland. This organization grew into a larger movement after World War I because its leaders believed that a worldwide organization was necessary to combat secular Zionist influences. *See also* Zionism.

Aktion (German; pl. *Aktionen*) A brutal roundup of Jews for mass murder by shooting or for deportation to forced labour, concentration and death camps.

Aliyah Bet (Hebrew) A clandestine movement established to bring Jewish immigrants without immigration permits to British Mandate Palestine before, during and after World War II. The name, which means "ascent B," differentiates the movement from the immigrants to whom the British granted permits. Aliyah Bet organized ships to pick up Jewish immigrants from different points on the European coast in order to make the perilous journey to Palestine. Many were turned back.

Allies The coalition of countries that fought against the Axis powers (Germany, Italy and Japan, and later others). At the beginning of World War II in September 1939, the coalition included France, Poland and Britain. After Germany invaded the USSR in June 1941 and the United States entered the war following the bombing of Pearl Harbor by Japan on December 7, 1941, the main leaders of the Allied powers became Britain, the USSR and the United

States. Other Allies included Canada, Australia, India, Greece, Mexico, Brazil, South Africa and China. *See also* Axis.

Aryanization The process of transferring businesses owned by Jews to non-Jews, or "Aryans," who were considered racially superior. From 1933 to 1938 in Nazi Germany, Jewish business owners were compelled to sell their devalued businesses to non-Jews at radically low prices, and in 1938, new regulations required Jews to transfer their businesses to non-Jews for almost no compensation. In other countries in occupied Europe, "Aryanization" laws were introduced to expropriate Jewish property and were implemented by governments that collaborated with the Nazis, such as Vichy France.

Association of Jews in Belgium (in French, Association des Juifs de Belgique; AJB) The association established by the German occupiers in November 1941 to consolidate all the Jews in Belgium under one administrative umbrella. Ostensibly created to oversee the welfare of the Jewish population in Belgium, the AJB's main tasks were in fact to implement the Germans' anti-Jewish measures, and the AJB ultimately facilitated the transport of Jews in Belgium to concentration camps and death camps. Like the Jewish Councils in occupied Eastern Europe, officials of the AJB faced difficult and complex moral decisions. Some members of the AJB were affiliated with the Belgian resistance and worked to rescue Jewish children through their orphanages and underground networks. *See also* Jewish Council, Netherlands.

Auschwitz (German; in Polish, Oświęcim) A Nazi concentration camp complex in German-occupied Poland about 50 kilometres from Krakow, on the outskirts of the town of Oświęcim, built between 1940 and 1942. The largest camp complex established by the Nazis, Auschwitz contained three main camps: Auschwitz I, a concentration camp; Auschwitz II (Birkenau), a death camp that used gas chambers to commit mass murder; and Auschwitz III (also called Monowitz or Buna), which provided slave labour for an industrial complex. In 1942, the Nazis began to deport Jews from almost every country in Europe to Auschwitz-Birkenau, where they were selected for slave labour or for death in the gas chambers. In mid-January 1945, close to 60,000 inmates were sent on a death march, leaving behind only a few thousand inmates who were liberated by the Soviet army on January 27, 1945. It is estimated that 1.1 million people were murdered in Auschwitz, approximately 90 per cent of whom were Jewish; other victims included Polish prisoners, Roma and Soviet prisoners of war.

Axis The coalition of countries that fought against the Allied powers (Britain, the United States, the USSR and others). At the beginning of World War II in September 1939, the coalition included Germany, Italy and Japan. Other Axis countries included Hungary, Romania, Slovakia, Bulgaria, Yugoslavia and Croatia. *See also* Allies.

Bachad (Hebrew; *Brith Chalutzim Dati'im*; Alliance of Religious Pioneers) An Orthodox Jewish pioneering youth movement started in Germany in 1928. The movement aimed to prepare young Jews for life in the Land of Israel by training them in religious ideals and agriculture, through training farms called hachshara. Training farms were first established in Germany before World War II and were later established in other countries, including Britain, Italy and the Netherlands, due to the emigration from Germany that followed Kristallnacht, after which all but two of the Bachad hachshara farms in Germany were closed. Bachad continued to operate after the war, with farms in Britain until 1962. *See also* Brith Hanoar; hachshara; Mizrachi; Zionism.

Brith Hanoar (Hebrew; Youth Alliance) An umbrella organization created by Jews affiliated with the German Mizrachi movement in 1928, originally based primarily in Poland and neighbouring countries. Brith Hanoar coordinated various other Mizrachi-affiliated religious Zionist youth organizations, and as a pioneering Zionist youth organization, it focused on preparing Jews for agricultural work in the Land of Israel. *See also* Bachad; hachshara; Mizrachi; Zionism.

British Mandate Palestine The area of the Middle East under British rule from 1923 to 1948 comprising present-day Israel, Jordan, the West Bank and the Gaza Strip. The Mandate was established by the League of Nations after World War I and the collapse of the Ottoman Empire; the area was given to the British to administer until a Jewish national home could be established. During this time, Jewish immigration was severely restricted, and Jews and Arabs clashed with the British and each other as they struggled to realize their national interests. The Mandate ended on May 15, 1948, after the United Nations Partition Plan for Palestine was adopted and on the same day that the State of Israel was declared.

canton An administrative subdivision within a country, similar to a province in Canada or state in the USA. In Switzerland, the term refers to a member state of the Swiss Confederation; Switzerland has twenty-six cantons.

cantor (in Hebrew, *chazzan*) A person who leads a synagogue congregation in songful prayer. The cantor might be professionally trained or a member of the congregation.

cattle cars Freight cars used to deport Jews by rail to concentration camps and death camps. The European railways played a key logistical role in how the Nazis were able to transport millions of Jews from around Europe to killing centres in occupied Poland under the guise of "resettlement." The train cars were usually ten metres long and often crammed with more than a hundred people in abhorrent conditions with no water, food or sanitation. Many Jews, already weak from poor living conditions, died in the train cars from suffocation or illness before ever arriving at the camps.

concentration camp A location in which people are held without recourse to rule of law, usually under difficult conditions. Under the Nazis, a large network of concentration camps was developed where prisoners — including Jews, Roma, homosexuals, political prisoners, prisoners of war, and others considered "undesirable" — were used as slave labour and provided with little food or other necessities, often resulting in death due to starvation, illness, exposure, beatings and execution. The camps were run by the SS, the elite police force of the Nazi regime that was responsible for security and for the enforcement of Nazi racial policies.

Dachau The first Nazi concentration camp to be established, in March 1933, located about sixteen kilometres northwest of Munich in southern Germany. At first Dachau held primarily political prisoners, but over the course of its existence, all the groups persecuted by the Nazis — Jews, Jehovah's Witnesses, homosexuals, Poles, Roma and others — were imprisoned there. From 1933–1945, approximately 190,000 prisoners were held in Dachau and its numerous subcamps, where they performed forced labour, mostly in the production of armaments for the German war effort. As the American forces neared the camp in April 1945, the Nazis forced 7,000 prisoners on a gruelling death march. It is estimated that over 40,000 people died in Dachau.

demarcation line The boundary between the northern part of France occupied by the Germans (Occupied Zone) and the southern Unoccupied Zone that was under the control of the French Vichy government until November 1942. *See also* Free Zone.

displaced persons camps Facilities set up by the Allied authorities and the United Nations Relief and Rehabilitation Administration (UNRRA) in October 1945 to resolve the refugee crisis that arose at the end of World War II. The camps provided temporary shelter and assistance to the millions of people — not only Jews — who had been displaced from their home countries as a result of the war and helped them prepare for resettlement. *See also* Red Cross; United Nations Relief and Rehabilitation Administration (UNRRA).

Eretz Yisrael (Hebrew; Land of Israel) The traditional Jewish name for Israel.

Free Zone (in French, zone libre) Also known as the Unoccupied Zone. The southern region of France that was under French sovereignty between June 1940 and November 1942, after which it was occupied by Germany. The seat of the collaborating French government was located in Vichy in the Free Zone, and its power was subordinated to the German occupiers.

Fortress Europe (in German, Festung Europa) During World War II and the Nazi occupation of much of Europe, the phrase was used by both the Allies and the Germans to refer to Continental Europe. In Nazi propaganda, the term referred especially to the fortifications of the Atlantic Wall, falsely assuring Germans that the continent was impenetrable to invasion by the Allies.

Gestapo (German; abbreviation of Geheime Staatspolizei, the Secret State Police) The Nazi regime's brutal political police that operated without legal constraints to deal with its perceived enemies. The Gestapo was formed in 1933 under Hermann Göring; it was taken over by Heinrich Himmler in 1934 and became a department within the SS in 1939. During the Holocaust, the Gestapo set up offices in Nazi-occupied countries and was responsible for rounding up Jews and sending them to concentration and death camps. They also arrested, tortured and deported those who resisted Nazi policies. *See also* SS.

hachshara (Hebrew; pl. *hachsharot*; preparation) Agricultural training program, and the farms used for this training, to prepare new immigrants for life in the Land of Israel. *See also* Bachad; kibbutz.

High Holidays (also High Holy Days) The period of time leading up to and including the Jewish autumn holidays of Rosh Hashanah (New Year) and Yom Kippur (Day of Atonement) that is considered a time for introspection and renewal. Rosh Hashanah is observed with synagogue services, the blowing of the shofar (ram's horn) and festive meals during which sweet foods, such as apples and honey, are eaten to symbolize and celebrate a sweet new year. Yom Kippur, a day of fasting and prayer, occurs eight days after Rosh Hashanah. *See also* Rosh Hashanah; Yom Kippur.

Jewish Council, the Netherlands (in Dutch, Joodse Raad) A Jewish representative group created by the German occupiers to administer Jewish life in the Netherlands and carry out German demands. Established in Amsterdam in February 1941, it became national by October 1941. The Jewish Council was completely subordinate to the German occupiers. Members of the Jewish Council, threatened with their own deportation, were forced to participate in collecting Jews to send to concentration camps and death camps. Like the Jewish Councils in occupied Eastern Europe, officials of the Joodse Raad faced difficult and complex moral decisions. *See also* Association of Jews in Belgium.

Jewish houses (in German, *Judenhäuser*) Designated areas or buildings where German Jews were forced to live, beginning as early as May 1939. The Jewish houses kept Jews segregated from the rest of the population and allowed the Nazi regime to seize Jewish properties. Jews were forced into crowded apartments or even shared rooms but were not as strictly confined as they were in the ghettos of Nazi-occupied Eastern Europe.

kibbutz (Hebrew; pl. kibbutzim) A collectively owned farm or settlement in Israel, democratically governed by its members. Among some of the Zionist youth movements in the Netherlands and elsewhere in Europe before and during World War II, the term was also used to refer to groups whose loyalty was to Palestine, although they did not yet live there. Members were organized into "kibbutz training groups" and some attended preparation training (hachshara) to immigrate to British Mandate Palestine. *See also* hachshara.

Kindertransport (German; children's transport) The British rescue operation to bring Jewish children out of Greater Germany after the Kristallnacht pogrom in November 1938. Between December 1938 and May 1940, the government-sanctioned but privately funded Kindertransport rescued approximately 10,000 German, Austrian and Czech children under the age of seventeen and placed them in British foster homes and hostels. Jewish organizations in Greater Germany provided important assistance in selecting children and preparing them for departure. Other Kindertransports brought children to different European countries, including the Netherlands, France, Sweden and Belgium, with about 1,500 children going to the Netherlands.

Kristallnacht (German; Night of Broken Glass) A series of antisemitic attacks instigated by the Nazi leadership that were perpetrated in Germany and the recently annexed territories of Austria and the Sudetenland on November 9 and 10, 1938. During Kristallnacht, ninety-one Jews were murdered, and between 25,000 and 30,000 Jewish men were arrested and deported to concentration camps. More than two hundred synagogues were burned down, and thousands of Jewish homes and businesses were ransacked, their windows shattered, giving Kristallnacht its name. This attack is considered a decisive turning point in the Nazis' systematic persecution of Jews.

Mizrachi (Hebrew; acronym of *merkaz ruchani*, spiritual centre) A religious Zionist movement founded in Vilna, Lithuania, in 1902, on the belief that the Torah is central to Zionism and that a Jewish homeland was essential to Jewish life. The movement's principles are encompassed in its slogan, "The land of Israel, for the people of Israel, according to the Torah of Israel." By the 1930s, numerous Mizrachi-affiliated youth groups existed throughout Europe, including several in the Netherlands and Belgium, many of which continued to operate after the war. Mizrachi and its main youth movement, Bnei Akiva, and the system of religious schools it established are still active internationally today. *See also* Bachad; Brith Hanoar; Zionism.

Mokum (Yiddish; place) Similar to the Hebrew word *makom*, place, a word used by Jews to refer to some cities in the Netherlands and Germany. The word is also used as a nickname for Amsterdam by non-Jewish Amsterdammers and others in the Netherlands, having first been part of Dutch slang and later losing the negative connotations of the slang term.

Nuremberg Laws The race laws passed by the Nazi government in September 1935 that legalized antisemitism and the separation of Jews from broader German society. Under the Reich Citizenship Law, German Jews were stripped of their citizenship and classified based on how much Jewish ancestry they had. Under the Law for the Protection of German Blood and Honour, marriages or sexual relations between Jews and Germans/"Aryans" were forbidden.

Orthodox Judaism The religious practice of Jews for whom the observance of Judaism is rooted in the traditional rabbinical interpretations of the biblical commandments. Orthodox Jewish practice is characterized by strict observance of Jewish law and tradition, such as the prohibition to work on the Sabbath and certain dietary restrictions.

Passover (in Hebrew, Pesach) An eight-day Jewish festival that takes place in the spring and commemorates the exodus of the Israelite slaves from Egypt. The festival begins with a lavish ritual meal called a seder, during which the story of the Exodus is told through the reading of a Jewish text called the Haggadah. During Passover, Jews refrain from eating any leavened foods. The name of the festival refers to God's "passing over" the houses of the Jews and sparing their lives during the last of the ten plagues, when the first-born sons of Egyptians were killed by God.

Red Cross A humanitarian organization founded in 1863 to protect the victims of war. During World War II, the Red Cross provided assistance to prisoners of war by distributing food parcels and monitoring the situation in prisoner-of-war (POW) camps and also provided medical attention to wounded soldiers and civilians. Today, in addition to the international body, the International Committee of the Red Cross (ICRC), there are national Red Cross and Red Crescent societies in almost every country in the world. *See also* displaced persons camps; United Nations Relief and Rehabilitation Administration (UNRRA).

Rosh Hashanah (Hebrew; New Year) The two-day autumn holiday that marks the beginning of the Jewish year and ushers in the High Holidays. It is celebrated with a prayer service and the blowing of the shofar (ram's horn), as well as festive meals that include symbolic foods such as an apple dipped in honey, which symbolizes the desire for a sweet new year. *See also* High Holidays.

SA (abbreviation of Sturmabteilung; "assault division," usually translated as "storm troopers") The SA served as the paramilitary wing of the Nazi Party and played a key role in Hitler's rise to power in the 1930s. Members of the SA were often called "Brown Shirts" for the colour of their uniforms, which distinguished them from Heinrich Himmler's all-black SS (Schutzstaffel) uniforms. The SA was effectively superseded by the SS after the 1934 purge within the Nazi party known as the "Night of the Long Knives." *See also* SS.

Sachsenhausen A concentration camp located north of Berlin, Germany, established in 1936. Its first inmates were political and criminal prisoners, as well as Roma and Sinti, Jehovah's Witnesses and homosexuals; several thousand Jewish men were sent to Sachsenhausen after the mass arrests of Kristallnacht in 1938. With the onset of the war, the camp began to hold Polish and Czech prisoners, as well as Soviet POWs, and in 1942 most of the Jewish prisoners were sent to Auschwitz-Birkenau. In the early years of the camp, prisoners were put to work building the camp and nearby facilities, but once the war started they began manufacturing military equipment for the war effort. Inmates of the camp were in constant danger of being tortured and killed at random, and the camp contained a killing facility that housed a gas chamber and crematorium. By January 1945, Sachsenhausen and its subcamps contained around 70,000–80,000 prisoners, but after prisoner transfers, death marches and killings, there were only about 3,000 remaining in the camp when the Soviets liberated it on April 22 of that year. Estimates put the total deaths at Sachsenhausen and its subcamps at 40,000–50,000. *See also* Kristallnacht.

Shabbat (in English, Sabbath; in Yiddish, Shabbes, Shabbos) The weekly day of rest beginning Friday at sunset and ending Saturday at nightfall, ushered in by the lighting of candles on Friday evening and the recitation of blessings over wine and challah (egg bread). A day of celebration as well as prayer, it is customary to eat three festive meals, attend synagogue services and refrain from doing any work or travelling.

SS (abbreviation of Schutzstaffel; Defence Corps) The elite police force of the Nazi regime that was responsible for security and for the enforcement of Nazi racial policies, including the implementation of the "Final Solution" — a euphemistic term referring to the Nazis' plan to systematically murder Europe's Jewish population. The SS was established in 1925 as Adolf Hitler's elite bodyguard unit, and under the direction of Heinrich Himmler, its membership grew from 280 in 1929 to 52,000 when the Nazis came to power in 1933, and to nearly a quarter of a million on the eve of World War II. SS recruits were screened for their racial purity and had to prove their "Aryan" lineage. The SS ran the concentration and death camps and also established the Waffen-SS, its own military division that was independent of the German army. *See also* Gestapo; SA.

tefillin (Hebrew; phylacteries) A pair of black leather boxes containing scrolls of parchment inscribed with Bible verses and traditionally worn by Jewish men on the arm and forehead at prescribed times of prayer as a symbol of the covenantal relationship with God.

Torah (Hebrew; instruction) The first five books of the Hebrew Bible, also known as the Five Books of Moses or Chumash, the content of which is traditionally believed to have been revealed to Moses on Mount Sinai; or, the entire canon of the twenty-four books of the Hebrew Bible, referred to as the Old Testament in Christianity. Torah is also broadly used to refer to all the teachings that were given to the Jewish people through divine revelation or even through rabbinic writings (called the Oral Torah).

United Nations Relief and Rehabilitation Administration (UNRRA) An international relief agency created at a 44-nation conference in Washington, DC, on November 9, 1943, to provide economic assistance and basic necessities to war refugees. It was especially active in repatriating and assisting refugees in the formerly Nazi-occupied European nations immediately after World War II. *See also* displaced persons camps; Red Cross.

Wehrmacht (German) The German army during the Nazi period.

Westerbork A transit and internment camp that was located in northeastern Netherlands in the province of Drenthe, near the town of Westerbork. Established by the Dutch government in October 1939 to hold Jewish refugees, the camp continued to be controlled by the Dutch authorities until formally being taken over by the German SS in July 1942. Between July 1942 and September 1944, close to 100,000 Jews were interned at Westerbork and, on more than one hundred transports, most were deported to the Nazi death camps and concentration camps of Auschwitz, Sobibor, Theresienstadt and Bergen-Belsen. Canadian forces liberated the remaining people from Westerbork on April 12, 1945.

Witte Brigade (Dutch; White Brigade) A Belgian resistance movement founded by Marcel Louette on July 23, 1940, in Antwerp. The group took on a national scope in 1941 and was active until the end of the war. After the Allied invasion in June 1944, the Witte Brigade supported the Allies through scouting and other activities, and helped them capture the port of Antwerp. Throughout its resistance to the Nazi occupation, the Witte Brigade suffered many losses, with hundreds being arrested, many of whom were sent to Nazi camps, including Louette, who was sent to Sachsenhausen but survived; four hundred of its members in total were killed.

Yehudi (Hebrew; from the Kingdom of Judah) A Biblical word for Jew.

yellow star The yellow badge or armband with the Star of David on it that many Jews in Nazi-occupied areas were forced to wear as an identifying mark of their lesser status and to single them out as targets for persecution. The Star of David, a six-pointed star, is the most recognizable symbol of Judaism.

Yom Kippur (Hebrew; Day of Atonement) A solemn day of fasting and repentance that comes eight days after Rosh Hashanah, the Jewish New Year, and marks the end of the High Holidays.

Zionism A movement promoted by the Viennese Jewish journalist Theodor Herzl, who argued in his 1896 book *Der Judenstaat* (The Jewish State) that the best way to resolve the problem of antisemitism and persecution of Jews in Europe was to create an independent Jewish state in the historical Jewish homeland of biblical Israel. Zionists also promoted the revival of Hebrew as a Jewish national language.

Photographs

Morris held by his father, Hermann Schnitzer. His grandmother, Baba Shoshi, is seated next to him, and his mother, Rosa, is standing. Bochum, 1922.

1 Morris's parents, Rosa and Hermann Schnitzer. Germany, circa 1920.
2 From left to right: Moishe (Morris) and his brothers, Benno and Edmund (Eddi). Germany, circa late 1920s.
3 Morris's mother, Rosa. Germany, mid-1930s.
4 Left to right: Hedwig Schrock, Morris's mother, Rosa, brother Benno and Morris at a spa on vacation. Germany, mid-1930s.

1 Morris's father, Hermann Schnitzer. Wattenscheid, Germany, circa late 1930s.

2 Morris's mother, Rosa Schnitzer. Wattenscheid, Germany, circa late 1930s.

3 Morris's brother Benno. Germany, circa late 1930s.

4 Morris's identification photo as Jan Van Capelle, his false identity. Brussels, July 1942.

1

2

1 Young Jews at the hachshara during the war, where they learned agricultural skills in preparation for life in the Land of Israel. Morris is hidden behind on the right, second row from the back. Franeker, the Netherlands, circa 1941. The Ghetto Fighters' House Museum, Israel/ The Photo Archive.

2 At the hachshara. Morris is standing behind, fifth from the left. Franeker, the Netherlands, circa 1941. The Ghetto Fighters' House Museum, Israel/ The Photo Archive.

Prison in Arbois, France, near the demarcation line, where Morris was detained.
Photo courtesy of Roger Gibey.

Morris's identification photo. Amsterdam, 1944.

Signature du porteur :

photo du porteur

Number: ....

SIGNALEMENT :

visage : _orale_
cheveux : _bruns foncés_
yeux : _bruns_
signes particuliers :
résidence : _Rheden_

Le porteur est accompagné de son épouse

née le

et de ses enfants au-dessous de l'âge de 15 ans.

.........., né le

, » »

, » »

, » »

, » »

, » »

, » »

4

IDENTITY
CERTIFICATE FOR ALIENS

Name and Christian names: _Schnitzer_
Morris Israel

Place of birth: _Bochum_

Date of birth: _February 4th 1922_

Of origine: _german_

Issued for travelling to
all over the world

THE HAGUE, _21 march 1947_

For the Minister,
(signature)

seal

This identity certificate is valid until _21 march 48_
and entitles the bearer to return to the Netherlands before that date. It cannot be renewed.

5

Here and opposite: pages from Morris's Dutch identification booklet required to leave the Netherlands to immigrate to Canada. 1947.

7798 NL. NL. *2937*

CANADA
Immigrant Visa

Authority: Ottawa 731952.

Issued at: The Hague

On: 8 April 1947

Valid for presentation at
Canadian Port of Entry within
_____ months from date

CANADIAN IMMIGRATION
3 APR 1947
THE HAGUE — HOLLAND

Op grond van verg. No. 412698 A/1

afgegeven

agenomen

Bankpapier: $ 50.= Koers 2.67°

geldswaarden:

Arnhem, 22 April 1947

REISBUREAU LISSONE - LINDEMAN N.V.

8

TRANSIT CERTIFICATE   APR 18 1947

No. 663

AMERICAN CONSULATE GENERAL
AMSTERDAM, NETHERLAND

I hereby certify that this passport
according to ... issued to me,
is about to pass through ... and States,
in transit to CANADA
via (port of entry) NEW YORK
(date of entry) ABOUT APRIL 30, 1947
and port of departure: PIER 88 NEW YORK
(date of departure) APRIL 30 5 FEBRUARY 1947

Not valid for more than one

James W. McElroy
Thomas W. McElroy
American Vice Consul

To Be Punished

Admitted at New York, N. Y.,
on MAY 3 19 1947 under Para-
graph 3 Section 3, Immigration
Act of 1924, for 2 weeks

Immigrant Inspector

9

Morris's brother Eddi and sister-in-law, Fay Schnitzer (née Reznick). Montreal, circa 1945.

Morris in Montreal. Circa late 1940s.

Morris and his wife, Leah (née Paltiel), at their wedding. Montreal, 1948.

1 Morris and his brother Eddi. Place unknown, circa late 1950s.
2 Morris at the Western Wall on his first trip to Israel. Jerusalem, 1968.
3 Morris working in a lab at the Soil Research Institute. Ottawa, 1967.

1

2

1 Morris and his wife, Leah, in Spain. Barcelona, circa 1972.
2 Morris and Leah. Mallorca, Spain, early 1980s.

Morris and his wife, Leah. Montreal, circa 1980s.

1

2

1 & 2 Morris on his return visit to the farm where he worked until liberation. Fexhe-le-Haut-Clocher, Belgium, 1981.

1

2

1 Morris standing in the farm's gate to which, almost forty years earlier, Monsieur Degive had given him the key, entrusting him to open it every morning and close it every night. Fexhe-le-Haut-Clocher, Belgium, 1981.

2 Morris on his trip back to the Netherlands. Franeker, 1981.

1   Morris and his grandson, Jan. Barcelona, 1988.
2   Morris and his brother Eddi in the Laurentian Mountains. Quebec, circa 1990s.

1

2

1 Morris, centre, becoming a Fellow of the Royal Society of Canada at Queen's University. Kingston, Ontario, 1991.

2 Morris, left, receiving the prestigious Wolf Prize in Agriculture in the Knesset. Jerusalem, March 24, 1996.

1–4 Letter and supporting documents sent to Morris's friend Jean Neyroud from a Swiss federal government archivist confirming that Morris Schnitzer, recorded as M. Schmitzer, and his companion, Menachem (Piefke) Levy, recorded as Erich Levy, are in the register of La Chaux-de-Fonds prison as having been detained on August 28, 1942. These "persons of Jewish religion or believed to be so" were "expelled to the French border."

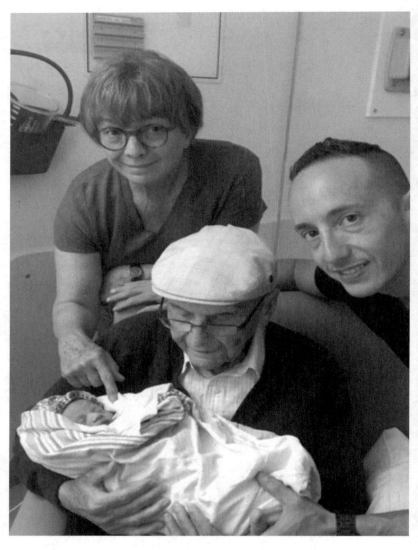

Four generations: Morris holding his great-grandson, Xavier, with grandson, Jan, and daughter, Eve. Ottawa, July 2017.

Morris and great-granddaughter Valentina. Ottawa, September 2019.

Index

The Azrieli Foundation was established in 1989 to realize and extend the philanthropic vision of David J. Azrieli, C.M., C.Q., M.Arch. The Foundation's mission is to support a wide spectrum of initiatives in education and research. The Azrieli Foundation is an active supporter of programs in the fields of education, the education of architects, scientific and medical research, and the arts. The Azrieli Foundation's many initiatives include: the Holocaust Survivor Memoirs Program, which collects, preserves, publishes and distributes the written memoirs of survivors in Canada; the Azrieli Institute for Educational Empowerment, an innovative program successfully working to keep at-risk youth in school; the Azrieli Fellows Program, which promotes academic excellence and leadership on the graduate level at Israeli universities; the Azrieli Music Project, which celebrates and fosters the creation of high-quality new Jewish orchestral music; and the Azrieli Neurodevelopmental Research Program, which supports advanced research on neurodevelopmental disorders, particularly Fragile X and Autism Spectrum Disorders.